A Pocket Guide to the
US Constitution

I confess that there are several parts of this constitution which I do not at present approve, but I am not sure I shall never approve them . . .

Thus I consent, Sir, to this Constitution because I expect no better, and because I am not sure, that it is not the best. The opinions I have of its errors, I sacrifice to the public good . . .

On the whole, Sir, I can not help expressing a wish that every member of the Convention who may still have objections to it, would with me, on this occasion doubt a little of his own infallibility, and to make manifest our unanimity, put his name to this instrument.

Benjamin Franklin, September 17, 1787
(final day of the Constitutional Convention)

A Pocket Guide

to the

US Constitution

WHAT EVERY AMERICAN

NEEDS TO KNOW

Second Edition

Andrew B. Arnold

Georgetown University Press ∞ Washington, DC

The publisher is not responsible for third-party websites or their content. URL links were active at time of publication.

Library of Congress Cataloging-in-Publication Data

Names: Arnold, Andrew Bernard, author.
Title: A pocket guide to the US constitution : what every American needs to know / Andrew B. Arnold.
Other titles: Pocket guide to the United States constitution
Description: Second edition. | Washington, DC : Georgetown University Press, 2018. | Includes bibliographical references and index.
Identifiers: LCCN 2017034205| ISBN 9781626165823 (hardcover : acid-free paper) | ISBN 9781626165588 (paperback : acid-free paper) | ISBN 9781626165595 (ebook)
Subjects: LCSH: Constitutional law—United States. | United States—Politics and government. | United States. Constitution.
Classification: LCC KF4550.Z9 A76 2018 | DDC 342.7302—dc23
LC record available at https://lccn.loc.gov/2017034205

♾ This book is printed on acid-free paper meeting the requirements of the American National Standard for Permanence in Paper for Printed Library Materials.

19   9 8 7 6 5 4 3

Printed in the United States of America

Cover design by Faceout Studio, Allison Nordin.
Cover art by Shutterstock and Getty Images.

Detailed Contents

Preface to the Second Edition

Unlike most pocket Constitutions, this one is designed to be *read*.

The Constitution is not so simple that it explains itself, nor so complex that only experts can understand it.

Political organizations like to hand out cheap pocket Constitutions with tiny lettering and zero explanation. Politicians like to wave them in the air. They seldom get read. This book is designed to get you started on the Constitution as a text and as a way to start understanding the American Constitutional system.

It contains a summary of what experts assume you already know. Experts examine the Constitution case by case, topic by topic, amendment by amendment. They assume their readers already know the structure, history, and assumptions behind the text itself. They talk in a shorthand of case names and nicknames.

This book is a quick guide that will help to make the vast literature on the Constitution more accessible.

- It is written in plain language.
- It will help you to read more in-depth books on the topic or to pursue online searches.
- It gives you the names of clauses and a standard numbering system (The Commerce Clause, for example, is Article 1, Section 8, Clause 3, or 1.8.3.)

It is written from the perspective of a historian, not a lawyer or a polemicist. It won't tell you what the Constitution

ought to say, nor what it ought to mean. It will tell you what
the Constitution says and what it has meant.

It is as complete as I can make it and still have it fit in your
pocket. It is as simple as I can make it and still have it be
complete.

and American political theory. The idea of being a good republican refers back to a Revolutionary-era ideal. Americans, republicanism said, were uniquely able to put public good ahead of private interest.

We the People of the United States

An earlier draft originally named the 13 states instead of "United States." But since the Constitution declared itself to be ratified once a mere nine of the 13 states approved it, this had to be changed. Any states that failed to ratify would be outside the new nation. By so ratifying, these united states continued the historical process of creating a nation called the "United States."

People

As suggested by the original draft's list of individual states, "people" refers to the people of individual states, united, as well as the people of the United States. It's easy to overstate this. The Declaration of Independence had already described Americans as a "people." Both John Adams and Patrick Henry referred to their state *and* the United States as their "country." Over time Americans have come to see themselves as a single diverse people, simultaneously members of their town, state, and nation (also ethnicity, party, religion, and sports team fanbase; the Constitution does not explicitly endorse a team or a sport).

Form a more perfect Union

This phrase suggests a wish to differentiate the Constitution from the then-governing Articles of Confederation. Since the Articles established a "perpetual union," this phrase became a way for pro-Union analysts during the Civil War to insist that the union of the Constitution also be perpetual.

Establish Justice . . . and our Posterity

These phrases name the Constitution's goals. The terms "common defence" and "general welfare" appear in section 8 of the Articles. The Congress named these goals in the resolution authorizing the Constitutional Convention. On May 30, 1787, the Convention decided that to achieve its assigned goals, it had to entirely replace the Articles. It was this crucial logical leap that led them to go beyond their original instructions from Congress. They could not merely make suggestions aimed at amending the Articles, they argued, and still achieve their assigned goals.

Do ordain and establish

This claim, combined with the ratification process, placed the Constitution above national and state legislatures. The new national government would rule by virtue of the sovereignty of "the people" and the states.

II.
Three Branches of Government

1. Legislative (Congress)
2. Executive (President)
3. Judicial (Courts)

The first three articles lay out conflicting powers and responsibilities for the three branches. This underlines a main point of the Constitution: It creates a government that, in its very structure, checks and balances the ability of any one part to become tyrannical. These branches battle with each other for power and function. They also battle for power with the other powerful elements of society: with the people, press, states, bureaucratic establishment, political parties, lobbyists, and private economic power.

The roles of the branches are defined in practice and custom as much as in the text of the Constitution. The Supreme Court spent its first decade establishing its role as the arbiter of the Constitution's meaning. The House of Representatives became more of a collection of local voices. The Senate has become more of a national voice. Executive powers expanded most greatly starting during the Civil War and the Gilded Age, again with the New Deal and World War II under Franklin D. Roosevelt, and then in the Civil Rights era.

Laws must be passed separately in the Senate and House of Representatives. The House and Senate then confer to negotiate any differences between their respective versions. The president can choose to sign or veto laws that clear both the House and Senate. Bureaucrats can enforce with gusto or indifference. The Court can invalidate. People and states resist or not.

All parties work within this set of constitutional and practical limitations. In the normal course of events, gaining the approval of all parties has become part of negotiations from the beginning. Bills are developed in full awareness of the legal context created by the Court's previous decisions. Public representatives in the House, Senate, executive branch, and states weigh in, as do private lobbyists and individuals.

ARTICLE 1 LEGISLATIVE

The framers were most familiar with the legislative branch and saw it as the first, most powerful branch of government. It was the section most firmly connected to the states and to the people. The Continental Congresses had managed the Revolutionary War and the new nation under the Articles of Confederation. Colonial legislatures had been the main form of government, successfully battling to control Royal governors.

Framer James Madison envisioned a national legislature that would be elected by the people of the individual states. It was to have veto power over state laws. Madison was forced to compromise on both goals. The House of Representatives was elected as he envisioned, by the people of each state. But representation and power in the Senate took place state by state. Nor was he able to achieve a veto on state laws.

Legislative powers were defined through the Enumerated Powers, and starting in the New Deal Era of the 1930s, they became centered on the power of Congress to regulate commerce between the states.

Section 1.1 The Legislature

Clause 1.1.1 Legislative Power Defined

All legislative Powers herein granted shall be vested in a Congress of the United States, which shall consist of a Senate and House of Representatives.

The First Branch of Government

The Founders saw the legislature as the leading branch of government. Congress had run the nation during the Revolutionary War and under the Articles of Confederation. Congress was most directly responsible to the people and to the states.

All legislative Powers . . . vested ("Delegation Doctrine")

The Constitution gives "all" legislative power to Congress. It was in part for this reason that the Court rejected the 1933 New Deal National Industrial Recovery Act (It ceded power to define "fair" codes without enough congressional oversight or definition of terms. *Schechter Poultry Corp. v. US* [1935]). Congress must oversee any bureaucratic agencies that it creates. Nevertheless, bureaucracies create their own centers of power.

Senate and House of Representatives

The split, bicameral legislature was a standard feature in most colonial state constitutions. People in each state elected their representatives, while state governments originally selected senators.

Great Compromise

Under the Articles, each state had the same vote in Congress. Delegates from larger states argued strongly that power in the new national legislature ought to be distributed according to population. In the so-called Great Compromise or Connecticut Compromise, the Convention agreed to distribute seats in the lower house according to the population of each state. Distribution of seats in the upper house, or Senate, was distributed equally among the states.

To James Madison and his supporters in the Constitutional Convention, this compromise made little sense. Why distribute power evenly among states of such wildly divergent size, population, and importance? Moreover, they argued, a nation had to be based on a single source of sovereignty: The new nation could base its legitimacy on the people. Or it could base its sovereignty on the states. They had a point. But the smaller states simply refused to accept anything less. Even in this, the smaller states were making a concession. Under the Articles of Confederation, the national government was based on equal representation between all of the states, no matter how small. Delaware's delegates had been explicitly instructed not to accept any change to that basis. Benjamin Franklin brokered this compromise, and after much bickering it was accepted.

Section 1.2 The House

Clause 1.2.1 Composition of House

The House of Representatives shall be composed of Members chosen every second Year by the People of the several States, and the Electors in each State shall have the Qualifications requisite for Electors of the most numerous Branch of the State Legislature.

The Electors in each State shall have the

This is one of the rare places where the Constitution defines the right to vote. It leaves the specifics to the states, but clause 1.4.1 lets Congress define those specifics.

By the People

The Court has used this term to judge the fairness of voting districts. State districts should be equal in population so each person's vote is worth roughly the same (*Wesberry v. Sanders* [1964]).

Congressional Districts

Unlike most political entities such as towns, counties, or states, congressional districts have a number, not a name. They change with the census every ten years as the nation's population shifts and the 435 House members of Congress are reapportioned among the states. The Court ruled in *League of United Latin American Citizens v. Perry* (2006) that states may redistrict more often than every ten years if they choose.

The Constitution left congressional districts up to the states to figure out. Smaller states such as Delaware at the founding and Wyoming today have only a single House member of Congress. For them, the entire state is the congressional district. Other state legislatures have divided up their states to create such districts. Until outlawed by the Apportionment Act of 1842, many states elected all of their representatives at-large, not from a specific district.

State House Districts and Congressional Districts

Pennsylvania's 1776 constitution originally treated cities, towns, and counties similar to the way the US Constitution treated the states. It assumed that if a town existed, it deserved representation in the state government. In later constitutions, however, similar to congressional districts, Pennsylvania divided the state into numbered districts. The current Pennsylvania constitution nevertheless states: "Unless absolutely necessary no county, city, incorporated town, borough, township or ward shall be divided in forming either a senatorial or representative district." This requirement has had little impact in recent years.

Few limits govern congressional districts. Nor do state districts generally align with congressional districts. The 200 Pennsylvania House districts are not combined to form the (currently) 20 congressional districts in the state. Historical political groups such as towns and cities have little relationship to state or congressional districts. Congressional districts may randomly overlap parts of several state districts.

Gerrymandering

The Constitution grants congressional districts within the states a national role through their elected representatives. Congressional districts are an odd sort of political entity. Most districts have little history and little political coherence. Yet the politics of towns, boroughs, villages, cities, states, and nations all share a history as citizens and as people with a coherent sense of place. The Court has largely seen "gerrymandering" (shaping districts to give one party or candidate a demographic advantage) to be a political issue, not a judicial one. But as modern geographical and polling data have become more precise, parties have been able to more drastically manipulate district boundaries for political advantage. The Court has put limits on the practice as it conflicts with other elements of American constitutionalism, especially regarding race. (See 14th Amendment, "Equal Protection and the Vote," below. See *Baker v. Carr* [1962]). More recently, District Courts have begun to weigh in on whether political gerrymandering can go too far. In *League of United Latin American Citizens v.*

Perry (2006), the Supreme Court rejected various ways to measure partisan fairness. A new standard called "efficiency gaps" may pass muster with the Court, however. In essence, it measures the difference between the number of registered party members in a state and the number of representatives it is able to elect. As this book goes to press, the Court has agreed to hear a case regarding Wisconsin's congressional districts.

Clause 1.2.2 Qualifications for Representatives

No Person shall be a Representative who shall not have attained to the Age of twenty five Years, and been seven Years a Citizen of the United States, and who shall not, when elected, be an Inhabitant of that State in which he shall be chosen.

What Qualifications Do You Need to Be a Member of the House?

A representative must 25 years old, an inhabitant of the state in which he or she is running, and a citizen of the US for seven years on Election Day. States may not create more qualifications for office, such as term limits (*US v. Thornton* [1995]).

Clause 1.2.3 Apportionment (Three Fifths Clause)

Representatives and direct Taxes shall be apportioned among the several States which may be included within this Union, according to their respective Numbers, which shall be determined by adding to the whole Number of free Persons, including those bound to Service for a Term of Years, and excluding Indians not taxed, three fifths of all other Persons. The actual Enumeration shall be made within three Years after the first Meeting of the Congress of the United States, and within every subsequent Term of ten Years, in such Manner as they shall by Law direct. The number of Representatives shall not exceed one for every thirty Thousand, but each State shall have at Least one Representative; and until such enumeration shall be made, the State of New Hampshire shall be entitled to chuse three, Massachusetts eight, Rhode Island and Providence Plantations one, Connecticut five, New York six, New Jersey four, Pennsylvania eight, Delaware one, Maryland six, Virginia ten, North Carolina five, South Carolina five, and Georgia three.

Representatives and direct Taxes shall be apportioned

More populous states were entitled to more votes in Congress, and they were entitled to more presidential electors.

Direct Taxes

The direct taxes provision was intended to spread the taxation burden equally among the people of the states. Note the early focus on treating states equally. The 16th Amendment finally severed apportionment of taxes from electoral power by permitting Congress to levy income taxes regardless of the census. See 1.9.4, below.

Three fifths of all other Persons

"Three fifths of all other Persons" refers to slaves. Slaves were to be counted as three-fifths of a person to apportion representatives, presidential electors, or the share of federal taxes among states. This was a split-the-difference compromise that pleased neither side. Slaveholders thought slaves should be worth a full person, to recognize the wealth that slaves represented to the slaveholder. Northerners thought slaves should be worth zero since they could not vote. (Why three-fifths? Why not half or three-quarters? The three-fifths ratio or "Federal Ratio" originated in a failed amendment to the Articles of Confederation in 1783.

Because of this, it was a familiar number to both sides, and they accepted it without much debate.)

The Three Fifths Clause often causes confusion. To be clear: It did not give slaves three-fifths of a vote. Slaves could not vote. The census counted all free persons as one full unit, or five-fifths of a person. The Three Fifths Clause counted each slave as three-fifths of a person. It was a way to apportion the number of members of Congress in the House of Representatives and the number of Electoral College electors.

The three-fifths number also gave more weight to each individual vote in slave states. It apportioned three-fifths of a vote for each slave but without adding more voters. Each slave therefore added power to the votes of white voters in states with slaves.

References to Slavery in the Constitution

The term "slavery" does not appear in the Constitution, but other references are made, such as three-fifths of "other Persons" (1.2.3), "such Persons" (1.9.1), and "No Person held to Service or Labour" (4.2.3). See also the prohibition on a capitation tax unless in proportion to apportionment of taxes and representatives (1.9.4). See also the last part of Article 5, which forbade any amendments to the articles that guaranteed slaveholder rights.

Indians not taxed

Those Indians who were not counted for taxes, were not counted for apportionment of House or presidential electors (see 1.8.3, Commerce Clause; 14th Amendment, Section 2). Indians gained citizenship in 1924, but states controlled the right to vote. Does the Constitution see Indians racially or as part of distinct political groupings? It's vague.

Term of ten Years

A national census must be held every ten years to accurately apportion representatives and presidential electors among the states as population shifts. This clause underlines the difficulty of creating a system of representation based on both individuals *and* individual states. State legislatures are responsible for drawing congressional districts.

Shall not exceed one for every thirty Thousand

The House met after ratification with 65 members (see above, Clause 1.2.3). After the first census, the Apportionment Act of 1792 allocated 105 members of the House of Representatives, setting each district at roughly 33,000 people. The Apportionment Act of 1810 raised that number to one member for every 35,000. By 1832, it had risen to 47,700 people.

The Constitution set a *maximum* level of representation: no *more* than one representative for every 30,000 citizens. In debate at the Convention, the original rule had been more precise: It was to be one representative for every 40,000 people. It was George Washington who stepped down from the chair to move that the number be lowered to 30,000.

To achieve that level of representation today, the House of Representatives would have to be structured very differently. The US now has over 300 million people. To divide by 30,000 would result in a House of 10,000 members. In the Reapportionment Act of 1929 Congress limited itself to 435 members, to be automatically reapportioned among all states after each census by the secretary of commerce. The US in 1920 had 106 million people. Each House member of Congress then represented an average of 244,000 people. In 2016 each of the 435 members of Congress represented an average of roughly 750,000 constituents. They represented as few as 523,000 people (Rhode Island's 2nd congressional

district. The representative from Wyoming, the state with
the lowest population, had 582,000 constituents.) They
represented as many as roughly 1 million constituents, as in
Montana's single district. If the US adopted the rule that the
size of congressional districts be decided by the population
of the smallest state, we would end up with a Congress of
roughly 515 members. A Congress set by the size of the
smallest district would be closer to 575 members. In neither
case would we get close to reaching George Washington's
standard of one member for every 30,000 residents.

(In comparison, in Great Britain each member of Parliament represents a constituency of roughly 70,000 electors,
or a total population of a little over 100,000. The 650 MPs of
the current House of Commons cannot easily fit into their
chambers at Westminster.)

> Clause 1.2.4 Vacancies
>
> When vacancies happen in the Representation from any
> State, the Executive Authority thereof shall issue Writs of
> Election to fill such Vacancies.

House Vacancies

House vacancies are filled by election, not appointment. If
the vacancy happens early in the two-year term, a special
election is generally held. If late in the term, states generally
wait until the next regular election. Specific rules differ from
state to state.

> Clause 1.2.5 Rules and Impeachment
>
> The House of Representatives shall chuse their Speaker
> and other Officers; and shall have the sole Power of
> Impeachment.

Rules

This clause gives the House of Representatives the right to organize itself and set its own rules.

Speaker and other Officers

The Speaker sets the agenda of the House. Under current law, he or she succeeds to the presidency if the president and vice president are incapacitated (see 2.1.6 and the 25th Amendment). The Speaker presides over joint sessions except when counting electoral votes (see 12th Amendment).

Power of Impeachment

The House first must pass articles of impeachment. It acts as a grand jury to decide if a trial is warranted. The Senate trial is based on those articles. See clause 1.3.6 for procedures. Clause 2.2.1b prohibits the president from using pardons to preempt impeachment. Section 2.4 defines who and for what reasons a federal official may be impeached.

Section 1.3 The Senate

> Clause 1.3.1 Definition of the Senate
>
> The Senate of the United States shall be composed of two Senators from each State, chosen by the Legislature thereof, for six Years; and each Senator shall have one Vote.

Two Senators from each State

This clause recognizes the historic sovereignty of the states as independent political entities. Every state has the same power in the Senate.

The "Rotten Borough" Problem

Periodic redistricting of congressional districts was a way to solve the "Rotten Borough" problem: What happens if an electoral district loses or gains population? There was no way to address this issue among the states. At the Constitutional Convention James Wilson pointed to the British town of Old Sarum. Once a bustling center of population, Old Sarum retained its right to send two members of Parliament even as its population dwindled to nearly zero. New population centers such as the city of Manchester received no new members until the Parliamentary Reform Act of 1832.

Framers who opposed equal representation among the states pointed to the Rotten Borough problem. On June 30, 1787, Founder James Wilson pointedly asked whether they were creating a government for "*men*, or for the imaginary beings called *states*." At the first census, Virginia had 12 times the population of the smallest state, New Hampshire. Today California has roughly 67 times the population of the smallest state, Wyoming.

Chosen by the Legislature thereof

The original decision to elect senators by state legislatures reflects the Great Compromise or Connecticut Compromise that based the new nation's sovereignty on the state as well as the people.

Popular Election of Senators

The 17th Amendment, passed in 1913, changed this clause to election by popular vote of each state.

Clause 1.3.2 Staggering Terms of Office

Immediately after they shall be assembled in Consequence of the first Election, they shall be divided as equally as may be into three Classes. The Seats of the Senators of the first Class shall be vacated at the Expiration of the second Year, of the second Class at the Expiration of the fourth Year, and of the third Class at the Expiration of the sixth Year, so that one third may be chosen every second Year; and if Vacancies happen by Resignation, or otherwise, during the Recess of the Legislature of any State, the Executive thereof may make temporary Appointments until the next Meeting of the Legislature, which shall then fill such Vacancies.

Perpetual Senate; Rules of Procedure

Unlike the House, where every member must be reelected every two years, only one-third of senators run for reelection at a time. Therefore, Senate rules remain in force while the House approves new rules for each new Congress. This is one reason why traditions and rules such as "holds," "courtesy," and "filibusters" that allow a minority of senators to prevent action have become such a dense tangle.

"Cloture" and "Filibuster"

In 1917 the Senate enacted a "cloture" rule to create a way to end debate. Originally invented to limit filibusters, it became a way to enable them. A senator can require a vote for "cloture" in order to begin the final vote on a bill. From 1917 to 1975, cloture required two-thirds of the senators present. A 1975 rule change required three-fifths of *all* senators (60 of 100). Starting in 2013, votes can be set by a majority vote for any appointments short of a Supreme Court nominee.

And if Vacancies happen by Resignation, or otherwise

The 17th Amendment, passed in 1913 and allowing for popular election of senators, allows states to provide for special election if they desire.

Clause 1.3.3 Qualifications for Senators

No Person shall be a Senator who shall not have attained to the Age of thirty Years, and been nine Years a Citizen of the United States, and who shall not, when elected, be an Inhabitant of that State for which he shall be chosen.

Qualifications for Senators

A senator must be 30 years old, a US citizen for nine years, and an inhabitant of the state by Election Day. (Before becoming vice president, Joe Biden was elected senator at age 29 but reached 30 by the time he was sworn in.)

Clause 1.3.4 Role of the Vice President

The Vice President of the United States shall be President of the Senate, but shall have no Vote, unless they be equally divided.

President of the Senate . . . unless they be equally divided

When the Senate is tied on a vote, the vice president casts the deciding vote. Outside of this clause, the vice presidency remains largely undefined. See also 1.3.5 Senate Officers and 1.3.6 Senate Impeachment Power.

Historical Development of Vice Presidency

George Washington saw the first vice president, John Adams, as a member of the legislature; the Senate saw him as a member of the executive branch. He thus had little to do. When Adams became president in 1796, his former opponent, Thomas Jefferson, used his time as vice president to attack him. The 12th Amendment tied president and vice president together.

Modern Vice Presidency

Recently, vice presidents have taken on a larger role, depending on agreements between the president and vice president. They have often become more of an "assistant president." Starting with Walter "Fritz" Mondale in 1976, vice presidents have gained more office space, staff, and executive branch functions.

> **Clause 1.3.5 Senate Officers**
>
> The Senate shall chuse their other Officers, and also a President pro tempore, in the Absence of the Vice President, or when he shall exercise the Office of President of the United States.

Senate President Pro Tempore

The Senate president pro tempore is third in line of succession under current law if the president, vice president, and Speaker of the House are incapacitated. Tradition places the senior member of the majority party in this position. It is largely ceremonial. See 25th Amendment.

Presiding over the Senate

In theory, the president pro tempore presides over the Senate. In practice, junior senators fill this job during routine business. This gives them the chance to learn the complex rules of the Senate and parliamentary procedure.

> **Clause 1.3.6 Senate Impeachment Power**
>
> The Senate shall have the sole Power to try all Impeachments. When sitting for that Purpose, they shall be on Oath or Affirmation. When the President of the United States is tried, the Chief Justice shall preside: And no Person shall be convicted without the Concurrence of two thirds of the Members present.

Senate Impeachment as Trial

Think of a Senate impeachment as a trial. Although the whiff of politics has always been part of such trials, the

Senate has consistently stopped short of allowing impeachments to take the place of elections.

When the President. . . the Chief Justice shall preside

Obviously, in this case, the vice president stands to gain the presidency if the current occupant is impeached. Therefore, he can't preside over the Senate during the trial.

> ### Clause 1.3.7 Limits to Impeachment Power
>
> Judgment in Cases of Impeachment shall not extend further than to removal from Office, and disqualification to hold and enjoy any Office of honor, Trust or Profit under the United States: but the Party convicted shall nevertheless be liable and subject to Indictment, Trial, Judgment and Punishment, according to Law.

Two presidents have been impeached, Andrew Johnson in 1868 and William Jefferson Clinton in 1998. Neither was convicted. Richard Milhous Nixon faced almost certain impeachment in 1974 but resigned before articles of impeachment could be passed.

Section 1.4 Elections, Meetings

> ### Clause 1.4.1 Senators and Representatives
>
> The Times, Places and Manner of holding Elections for Senators and Representatives, shall be prescribed in each State by the Legislature thereof; but the Congress may at any time by Law make or alter such Regulations, except as to the Places of chusing Senators.

State versus Congressional Control over Elections

This clause sets up a never-ending battle between state and federal power. The Supreme Court also weighed in on the question of fair election rules, especially under the 14th

Amendment's guarantee of equal protection of the laws and after the Voting Rights Act of 1965.

> **Clause 1.4.2 Sessions of Congress**
>
> The Congress shall assemble at least once in every Year, and such Meeting shall be on the first Monday in December unless they shall by Law appoint a different Day.

On the first Monday in December

The 20th Amendment, Section 2, changed this date to January 3 to better fit with the new swearing-in dates of the president and vice president (January 20).

Section 1.5 Membership, Rules, Journals, Adjournment

> **Clause 1.5.1 Quorum, Attendance, Seating**
>
> Each House shall be the Judge of the Elections, Returns and Qualifications of its own Members, and a Majority of each shall constitute a Quorum to do Business; but a smaller Number may adjourn from day to day, and may be authorized to compel the Attendance of absent Members, in such Manner, and under such Penalties as each House may provide.
>
> **Clause 1.5.2 Rules, Punishment, Expulsion**
>
> Each House may determine the Rules of its Proceedings, punish its Members for disorderly Behaviour, and, with the Concurrence of two thirds, expel a Member.

Bylaws to Govern Congress

Congress is largely free to develop rules regarding member conduct. See "Cloture" and "Filibuster" under 1.3.2, above.

Expulsion of a Member

Powell v. McCormack (1969) ruled that Congress could only expel a member by an explicit two-thirds vote. It could expel members only if they failed to meet citizenship, age, and residency requirements. Before then, most refusals to seat elected members of Congress related to white, Southern representatives who won office through racial violence after the Civil War.

> Clause 1.5.3 Openness, Secrecy, Roll Call Votes
>
> Each House shall keep a Journal of its Proceedings, and from time to time publish the same, excepting such Parts as may in their Judgment require Secrecy; and the Yeas and Nays of the Members of either House on any question shall, at the Desire of one fifth of those Present, be entered on the Journal.

Journal of its Proceedings

The journals list votes held and, when one-fifth of those present demand it, the results of roll call votes. The roll call vote puts each senator or representative on record and, given the difficulty of the process, also serves to delay proceedings.

Secrecy

The House made its sessions open, except for special purposes. The Senate has been more secretive, keeping its sessions closed until the 1790s, and keeping committee meetings closed until the rule reforms of the mid-1970s.

Congressional Record

The *Congressional Record* includes debates and statements entered into the record. Be forewarned, however, that representatives and senators retain the right to edit their remarks before publication, so what you read may not be precisely what they said.

> Clause 1.5.4 Adjournment and Place of Meeting
>
> Neither House, during the Session of Congress, shall, without the Consent of the other, adjourn for more than three days, nor to any other Place than that in which the two Houses shall be sitting.

Adjournment

House and Senate must agree on a date of adjournment to end a given legislative session. Both have the independent power to end their sessions for the day or for up to three days. They are not permitted to independently move the seat of government. If they cannot agree to a time of adjournment, the president may adjourn them, though no president has ever done so. See 2.3.1b, below.

Section 1.6 Compensation

> Clause 1.6.1 Payment and Immunities
>
> The Senators and Representatives shall receive a Compensation for their Services, to be ascertained by Law, and paid out of the Treasury of the United States. They shall in all Cases, except Treason, Felony and Breach of the Peace, be privileged from Arrest during their Attendance at the Session of their respective Houses, and in going to and returning from the same; and for any Speech or Debate in either House, they shall not be questioned in any other Place.

Compensation. . . Treasury of the United States

Pay for Congress is determined by law. They are *not* paid by state treasuries, as they had been under the Articles. Congress represents not only the states but the nation. The 27th

Amendment prevents a Congress from raising its own pay, though it can raise the pay of the Congress that follows it.

Privileged from Arrest during their Attendance

There is little to this privilege. Members are still liable for any crime worth bragging about. They can be sued during a session.

Privileged from arrest . . . for any Speech or Debate

Congressmen cannot be sued for libel for anything they say when doing the work of legislating. They can, however, be sued for statements made outside of that narrow function. Nor may any of their legislative functions be used as evidence against them in any court proceedings.

Clause 1.6.2 Incompatibility and Emoluments

No Senator or Representative shall, during the Time for which he was elected, be appointed to any civil Office under the Authority of the United States, which shall have been created, or the Emoluments whereof shall have been encreased during such time; and no Person holding any Office under the United States, shall be a Member of either House during his Continuance in Office.

Emoluments Clause

No senator or representative may be appointed to any office created while he or she was in office, or to any office that had increased its pay, pensions, or other "emoluments" during that period. See 1.9.8 for more on emoluments.

Incompatibility Clause

Legislators may not hold any other federal offices while in office. They cannot be military officers, for example, or serve in both houses, as judges or federal bureaucrats, or as elected officials such as president. The point of this provision was to maintain the separation of powers between the branches of government and to prevent favored lawmakers from receiving lucrative make-work jobs. Spouses and relatives of lawmakers may take jobs in the executive branch, but scandals have arisen when such jobs have proved to be obviously fake.

Work-Arounds

In some cases lawmakers have been appointed to jobs for which Congress had just raised the pay. In such cases, presidents have requested that the pay be lowered for the new appointee to the old level to comply with this provision.

Section 1.7 Passage of Bills into Law

Clause 1.7.1 Tax Laws

All Bills for raising Revenue shall originate in the House of Representatives; but the Senate may propose or concur with Amendments as on other Bills.

All Bills for raising Revenue shall originate in the House

This provision was originally conceived as part of the Great Compromise (see 1.1.1). It was intended to be a gesture to the larger-population states that (it was assumed) would dominate in the House. It might have had slightly more impact in its original form, when the Senate was also prohibited from adding amendments to revenue bills. Even in its original form, James Madison argued that it added little since the upper house could still hold up non-money bills in order to negotiate.

What Power Does the House Gain from This?

The House gains little or no power from this. There isn't much practical difference between originating a bill, after all, and adding an amendment. In practice, the House and Senate negotiate revenue-raising bills in largely the same manner as any other bill. It is more important as an artifact of how the Founding Fathers worked out the relative functions of House and Senate. (Elbridge Gerry referred to this issue in a letter, January 21, 1788, Max Farrand, *The Records of the Federal Convention of 1787*, 3:263.)

Clause 1.7.2 Presentment Clause

Every Bill which shall have passed the House of Representatives and the Senate, shall, before it becomes a Law, be presented to the President of the United States; If he approve he shall sign it, but if not he shall return it, with his Objections to that House in which it shall have originated, who shall enter the Objections at large on their Journal, and proceed to reconsider it. If after such Reconsideration two thirds of that House shall agree to pass the Bill, it shall be sent, together with the Objections, to the other House, by which it shall likewise be reconsidered, and if approved by two thirds of that House, it shall become a Law. But in all such Cases the Votes of both Houses shall be determined by yeas and Nays, and the Names of the Persons voting for and against the Bill shall be entered on the Journal of each House respectively. If any Bill shall not be returned by the President within ten Days (Sundays excepted) after it shall have been presented to him, the Same shall be a Law, in like Manner as if he had signed it, unless the Congress by their Adjournment prevent its Return, in which Case it shall not be a Law.

Veto and Difficulty of Passing Bills

Keep in mind the difficulty of passing a bill through the procedures of both houses and then reconciling the two versions. It's torturous. Few bills survive the process. Because of this, the veto returns a bill to the final voting stage. That way it can be quickly passed by two-thirds vote overriding the veto. Or not.

Pocket Passage

If the president fails to sign a bill while Congress is in session, it becomes a law after ten days.

Pocket Veto

If Congress approves a bill but adjourns fewer than ten days later, the president can choose to ignore it. In such a case, the bill does *not* become law, and Congress has to wait until its next session and then be forced to start the entire lengthy process over again (unlike in a normal veto).

Pro Forma Sessions

To prevent pocket vetoes (and to prevent the president from making "recess appointments" without the "advice and consent" of the Senate), Congress in recent years has stayed in "pro forma" session. See *National Labor Relations Board v. Noel Canning* (2014) for the Court's detailed ruling on the scope and purpose of presidential recess appointments. In short, the Court ruled that the pro forma sessions in which the Senate claims it is in session (even if without an actual quorum of senators) is sufficient to block any recess appointments.

Line-Item Veto

The Court ruled that the president may not decide to accept part of some laws and not others. Therefore, the so-called line-item veto was ruled unconstitutional. See *Clinton v. City of New York* (1998).

Presidential Signing Statements

In these statements, presidents can give their interpretation of a law, including whether or not they consider aspects to be unconstitutional, and the extent to which they intend to enforce it. The Court has yet to rule definitively on the extent to which these statements violate the present-ment clause. Are they like a line-item veto in that they approve part of a bill and not another? Are they examples of presidential lawmaking? Or are they simply presidential intentions regarding *how* he or she will "faithfully execute" the laws?

> Clause 1.7.3 All Bills, Full Legislative Process
>
> Every Order, Resolution, or Vote to which the Concur-rence of the Senate and House of Representatives may be necessary (except on a question of Adjournment) shall be presented to the President of the United States; and before the Same shall take Effect, shall be approved by him, or being disapproved by him, shall be repassed by two thirds of the Senate and House of Representatives, according to the Rules and Limitations prescribed in the Case of a Bill.

Every Order . . . (Primacy of Legislative Process)

In this complex section, the framers attempted to ensure that all federal authority would be exercised *only* by going through the entire legislative process. They wished to prevent both Congress and the president from bypassing checks and balances. The vast expansion of government institutional power in the congressional and presidentially controlled bureaucracy has tested this clause to the limit.

Section 1.8 Enumerated Powers of Congress

Enumerated Powers

This is the name given to the 18 powers "enumerated" (listed) in sections 1.8.1 to 1.8.18. "Strict construction" thinkers such as Thomas Jefferson insisted that these were properly the *only* powers ceded to Congress. (His views changed as president.) All other powers are reserved to the states (see the 10th Amendment). "Loose construction" thinkers such as Alexander Hamilton disagreed. See 1.8.18 "Necessary and Proper," below.

> Clause 1.8.1 Taxes, Debt, Welfare, Uniformity
>
> The Congress shall have Power To lay and collect Taxes, Duties, Imposts and Excises, to pay the Debts and provide for the common Defence and general Welfare of the United States; but all Duties, Imposts and Excises shall be uniform throughout the United States;

"Loose Construction"

See the Necessary and Proper Clause (1.8.18). In practice, in order for Congress to accomplish the goals of the first 17 powers listed, it claimed the right to do whatever was "necessary and proper" to accomplish them.

Lay and collect Taxes

This addressed a major limit on the power of the national government under the Articles. Under the Articles, the national government depended on the state governments to pay their portion of taxes but had no mechanism to force them to do so. Under the Constitution, the national government could enact taxes on individuals of the states.

Shall be uniform

Clause 1.2.3 requires taxes to be apportioned evenly according to population among the states. See also the 16th Amendment, legalizing federal income taxes, which overturned this clause. This clause should underline the more state-oriented nature of the Constitution when passed. See Capitation Tax, 1.9.4.

> Clause 1.8.2 Congress and Credit
>
> To borrow money on the credit of the United States;

Congress's Power to Borrow

The new nation needed the kind of credit that it had never established under the Articles. Alexander Hamilton hoped to use payment of the Revolutionary War debt to help concentrate the nation's sparse wealth in order to create investment capital. This policy recreated the situation that had motivated rural Pennsylvania to join the Revolution in 1776 and then helped to motivate many of those same people to join the Whiskey Rebellion against the new constitutional power to tax in the 1790s.

> Clause 1.8.3 Commerce Clause
>
> To regulate Commerce with foreign Nations, and among the several States, and with the Indian Tribes;

Commerce Clause Summary

Starting in 1937, during the Great Depression, the Court began to grant Congress almost unlimited power to pass economic regulations. For example, Congress used its power under the Commerce Clause to enforce the Civil Rights Act of 1965. See 2c, below, "As Authority for Civil Rights Laws."

Outline of Commerce Clause History

1. [with foreign Nations]
2. [among the several States]
   a. Broad Authority to Congress (Early National Period)
   b. Contradictory Precedents (Gilded/Progressive Era)
      i.   Prohibited Regulation of Indirect Commerce (Manufacturing, Mining)
      ii. Permitted Regulation of Stream of Commerce (Stockyards, Railroads)
      iii. No Social Legislation (Wages and Hours)
      iv. Prohibits Congress from Ceding Power to Regulate to the Executive Branch (Delegation Doctrine)
   c. Almost Unlimited Power over Commerce (New Deal)
      i. Labor Unions: Collective Worker Rights and Collective Property Rights
      ii. As Authority for Civil Rights Laws
   d. Post-1995 Limits on Congress
3. [with Indian Tribes]

With foreign Nations

See 2.2.2a for the president's power to make treaties with the advice and consent of the Senate. The key here is that commerce with foreign nations is supposed to be a matter for the national government, not the states.

Among the several States

When does commerce in one state join the commerce of another state enough to qualify as "among" the states under this enumerated power? What commerce is "intrastate" (solely within the state) and what commerce qualifies as "interstate?" If commerce is intrastate, then it is not subject to this enumerated power of Congress. If commerce is interstate, then it is. The question of what kinds of economic activity count under this section is answered more by the Court's policy aims than by any set definition.

In the early national period, the Marshall Court wanted to expand Congress's power and to prevent states from creating artificial barriers to trade. Therefore, it defined more economic activity as "interstate commerce." But from roughly 1880 to 1937, the Court wanted to prevent Congress from regulating the new industrial economy. Therefore, it narrowed the definition of interstate commerce. In the New Deal era, starting in 1937, the Court wanted to expand Congress's power to regulate the economy. Therefore, it vastly widened the definition of interstate commerce to include almost all economic activity. By 1965, Congress passed civil rights legislation almost entirely based on its power to regulate commerce. More recently, the Court has put limits on what Congress can define as economic activity. (See below for details.)

a. Broad Authority to Congress (Early National Period)
    The Court gave Congress broad power over commerce in early cases. In *Gibbons v. Ogden* (1824), it ruled that New York could not grant a monopoly to a steamboat company. The Court wanted to stop states from interfering in commerce, especially (as in *Gibbons*) activity that crossed state lines. The Federalist Marshall Court wished to expand national power.

b. Contradictory Precedents (Gilded/Progressive Era)
    Commerce at the dawn of the 1900s linked states in ways that the framers in 1787 never expected. In response, the Court developed four contradictory sets of precedents. In the New Deal era it would expand the second of these, allowing most economic regulations, no matter how tenuous the thread of their interstate connection.

    i. Prohibited Regulation of Indirect Commerce (Manufacturing, Mining).
        It prohibited regulation of business "indirectly" related to interstate commerce. *US v. EC Knight* (1895).

Congress could not regulate sugar refining (nor mines or factories). See also *Carter v. Carter Coal Co.* (1936).

ii. Permitted Regulation of Stream of Commerce (Stockyards, Railroads).

It let Congress regulate some forms of commercial activity, even within a state, that it saw as part of the "stream of commerce." This included Chicago meatpacking stockyards, where the consumers were largely on the East Coast (*Swift v. US* [1905]), and railroads (*Shreveport Rate Case* [1914]; and *Interstate Commerce Commission v. Atchison T & SF R. Co.* [1893]).

iii. No Social Legislation (Wages and Hours).

The Court prohibited regulations that seemed to go outside of narrow economic purposes, invalidating a ban on child labor, maximum hours, minimum wages, and most safety regulations (*Hammer v. Dagenhart* [1918]). (See also the 14th Amendment, Substantive Due Process; and *Lochner v. New York* [1905].)

iv. Prohibits Congress from Ceding Power to Regulate to the Executive Branch (Delegation Doctrine).

The Court ruled that the Congress could not constitutionally cede its power to regulate commerce to unelected agencies. The Constitution gave *all* such power to Congress. The Court saw agency regulations as requiring the full legislative process. See 1.1.1 "Legislative Power Defined," and 1.7.3, "All Bills, Full Legislative Process."

c. Almost Unlimited Authority over Commerce (New Deal)

In 1937 the Court expanded the definition of "stream of commerce." See above, 2bii. It began to defer more to Congress's judgment in making economic regulations (*National Labor Relations Board v. Jones & McLaughlin Steel* [1937]).

i. Labor Unions: Collective Worker Rights and Collective Property Rights

The National Labor Relations Act, or Wagner Act, passed in 1935, formalized union institutions and activism under federal law. Unions had long existed, but prior to 1937 the Court prohibited most federal laws regulating labor. Prior to the Wagner Act almost all labor union activism was prohibited as criminal conspiracy under common law. See *Commonwealth v. Pullis* (1806) (The "Cordwainers Case"); and *Commonwealth v. Hunt* (1842). Using criminal conspiracy as precedent, judges routinely issued injunctions prohibiting nearly all strike-related union activities.

ii. As Authority for Civil Rights Laws

Congress used the Commerce Clause to pass the Civil Rights Act of 1964 that prohibited racial discrimination in private enterprises. (See commentary on Privileges or Immunities under the 14th Amendment for why Congress couldn't directly claim the power to outlaw racial discrimination.) See *Heart of Atlanta Motel v. US* (1964).

d. Post-1995 Limits on Congress

In *US v. Lopez* (1995) the Court refused to accept Congress's reasoning that regulating guns in schools was acceptable as a regulation of commerce. See also *US v. Morrison* (2000). The Court rejected similar arguments regarding federal regulation of marijuana in *Gonzales v. Raich* (2005). The power of Congress under this clause remains in flux after *NFIB v. Sebelius* (2012).

With Indian Tribes

This clause sees the Indian Tribes as political entities. In *Cherokee Nation v. Georgia* (1831) the Court ruled that tribes were "domestic dependent nations" under Congress. In *Worcester v. Georgia* (1832) the Court voided Georgian laws on Cherokee land. The ruling went unenforced. The Cherokees were marched out of Georgia in what became known as the Trail of Tears.

Indian Sovereignty

The Court ruled in *California v. Capazon Band of Mission Indians* (1987) that states could not outlaw gambling on tribal land if they permitted it elsewhere. This ruling has been enforced through the Preemption Doctrine, in which national laws preempt state laws in the Supremacy Clause, Article 6, section 2. Congress regulates Indian gambling. Indian tribes today are at most semisovereign under Congress.

> Clause 1.8.4 Naturalization, Bankruptcy
>
> To establish an uniform Rule of Naturalization, and uniform Laws on the subject of Bankruptcies throughout the United States;

Uniform Rules for Naturalization and Bankruptcies

Here the emphasis is on national standards for citizenship and treatment of debtors across all states. Congress first created a bankruptcy act in 1898, with major amendments in 1938 and 1978. The 14th Amendment established citizenship for "all persons" born in America.

> Clause 1.8.5 Money, Standard Weights, and Measures
>
> To coin Money, regulate the Value thereof, and of foreign Coin, and fix the Standard of Weights and Measures;

To coin Money

The Constitution includes a more sophisticated set of federal monetary powers than implied by this clause alone. It appeared to straightforwardly limit Congress to regulat-

ing the quantity and quality of precious metal in silver and
gold coin. But in combination with the Commerce Clause
(1.8.3) and the power to borrow money (1.8.2), it also gave
Congress the power to issue paper money and to require its
acceptance as legal tender.

> Clause 1.8.6 Counterfeiting
>
> To provide for the Punishment of counterfeiting the Securi-
> ties and current Coin of the United States;

Counterfeiting

The power to regulate commerce and money meant Congress needed the power to prevent counterfeiting.

> Clause 1.8.7 Post Offices and Post Roads
>
> To establish Post Offices and post Roads;

1st Amendment versus Congressional Power

Congress argued that the power to establish post offices
gave it the right to forbid mailing subversive or salacious
materials. It applied this power freely, especially during and
after World War I. See *US ex rel Milwaukee Social Democratic Publishing Co. v. Burleson* (1921). In *Hannegan v. Es-
quire* (1946) the Court ruled that 1st Amendment freedom
of speech forbids Congress from using this power to impose
its taste. Congress may prohibit use of the mail for fraud.
Public Clearing House v. Coyne (1904).

Pullman Strike

When a railroad strike against the Pullman Car Company
also stopped some US mail delivery, the Court allowed an
injunction under this power against the entire strike effort.
In re Debs (1895).

Clause 1.8.8 Copyright

To promote the Progress of Science and useful Arts, by securing for limited Times to Authors and Inventors the exclusive Right to their respective Writings and Discoveries;

Copyright, Patent, Trademark

The point of this clause is named in the first few words: "To promote the Progress." Congress has broad power to promote creative efforts by giving creators a set of exclusive rights to achieve these aims. The Court's involvement has largely been limited to defining what is meant by the key terms: promotion, progress, invention, and discovery. Recently in *Eldred v. Ashcroft* (2003) the court ruled that Congress could extend copyright protection forever, as long as each extension was "limited" in time.

Clause 1.8.9 Inferior Courts

To constitute Tribunals inferior to the supreme Court;

Constitute Tribunals

See 3.1.1 for more on such courts. Congress has also created specialized "Article 1" Courts under this clause.

Clause 1.8.10 High Seas and Laws of Nations

To define and punish Piracies and Felonies committed on the high Seas, and Offenses against the Law of Nations;

Plenary Power

Congress is granted this power exclusively. Individual states cannot take it upon themselves to set up separate rules.

International Law

This clause gives Congress the power to set up courts to try violations of international law such as the laws of war.

> Clause 1.8.11 To Declare War
>
> To declare War, grant Letters of Marque and Reprisal, and make Rules concerning Captures on Land and Water;

To declare War

The Court has refused to referee in the battle between the president's executive function as commander in chief of the armed forces and Congress's power to formally declare war. In practice, presidents generally make war as an extension of their power over foreign affairs and dare Congress to stop them, mostly through its control over money necessary to deploy the armed forces.

Grant Letters of Marque and Reprisal

This clause grants Congress the sole right to issue what were essentially licenses for piracy or "privateers" beyond the "marque" or border of the nation. A common practice in the eighteenth century, this is no longer a legal practice under international law. (Congress issued such a letter during World War II to allow blimps to patrol for submarines.)

To . . . make Rules concerning Captures

This clause allows Congress sole right to make rules for seizing enemy property.

> Clause 1.8.12 Army
>
> To raise and support Armies, but no Appropriation of Money to that Use shall be for a longer Term than two Years;

To raise and support Armies

This clause gives Congress the right to impose a draft (as the states did under the Articles). The limit of two years on appropriations addresses the fear of standing armies.

> Clause 1.8.13 Navy
>
> To provide and maintain a Navy;

Navy

The Navy was seen as less dangerous to liberties than a standing army and more in need of long-term investment.

> Clause 1.8.14 Military Code
>
> To make Rules for the Government and Regulation of the land and naval Forces;

To make Rules for . . . the land and naval Forces

The military has separate judicial processes.

> Clause 1.8.15 Control of Militia
>
> To provide for calling forth the Militia to execute the Laws of the Union, suppress Insurrections and repel Invasions;
>
> Clause 1.8.16 Division of Militia with States
>
> To provide for organizing, arming, and disciplining the Militia, and for governing such Part of them as may be employed in the Service of the United States, reserving to the States respectively, the Appointment of the Officers, and the Authority of training the Militia according to the discipline prescribed by Congress;

Control of Militia

Clauses 1.8.15 and 1.8.16 give Congress some power over the individual state militias. The 2nd Amendment reassured the states that this clause was not a sneaky way to consolidate armed power in national hands.

> Clause 1.8.17 District of Columbia
>
> To exercise exclusive Legislation in all Cases whatsoever, over such District (not exceeding ten Miles square) as may, by Cession of particular States, and the Acceptance of Congress, become the Seat of the Government of the United States, and to exercise like Authority over all Places purchased by the Consent of the Legislature of the State in which the Same shall be, for the Erection of Forts, Magazines, Arsenals, dockyards and other needful Buildings;

Washington, District of Columbia

The District of Columbia was first established by Congress in 1790. The decision to create a separate district gave the new federal government independence from any individual state. It was located in Maryland and Virginia as part of the compromise that nationalized state Revolutionary War debts. Virginia's land was returned in 1846. Congress first met in Washington, DC, in November 1800.

Self-Government in Washington, DC

This increasingly large city slowly gained powers of self-government since 1967. It has one delegate to the US Congress but no *voting* representation in Congress. Its residents were first able to vote for president through the 23rd Amendment (1961). Congress allows the District limited self-rule.

> Clause 1.8.18 Necessary and Proper
>
> And To make all Laws which shall be necessary and proper for carrying into Execution the foregoing Powers, and all other Powers vested by this Constitution in the Government of the United States or in any Department or Officer thereof.

Necessary and Proper, the "Elastic" or "Coefficient" Clause

This clause expands federal power by allowing Congress to pass any laws that it deems necessary to enact the preceding list of enumerated powers.

Strict Construction: Necessary and Proper

One view of this clause sees it as strictly limiting federal power. Thomas Jefferson, a proponent of limited national power, insisted to George Washington that this clause allowed Congress to make *only* those laws that were both necessary *and* proper. That is, he saw "absolutely" implied before the word "necessary," and the words "for survival" after it. This view would have limited Congress's powers to those "expressly" enumerated, as in the Articles.

"Loose" Construction

Alexander Hamilton's interpretation came to rule, mostly. He insisted to George Washington that the term "necessary and proper" did not limit the power of Congress but rather expanded it to any laws implied by the foregoing enumerated powers. Thus, this clause came to be called "elastic" because it could be broadly interpreted by Congress to include powers not specifically mentioned but important to carrying out enumerated powers. "Necessary" here means "whatever powers were needed in order to accomplish the functions of government authorized by the Constitution." As with so much in the Constitution, the clause's elasticity depends on the political power and restraint of those doing the stretching.

Court's Ruling on Necessary and Proper

In *McCulloch v. Maryland* (1819), the Court agreed with Hamilton. It ruled that the term "necessary and proper" gave Congress the power to make laws implied by the foregoing powers. It ruled that the enumerated powers allowing Congress to regulate interstate commerce, raise taxes, and borrow money implied the power to create a national bank. Moreover, combined with the Supremacy Clause, such a power made Maryland's law taxing the National Bank Branch in Baltimore unconstitutional.

Section 1.9 Limits on Congress

Clause 1.9.1 Right to Slave Trade

The Migration or Importation of such Persons as any of the States now existing shall think proper to admit, shall not be prohibited by the Congress prior to the Year one thousand eight hundred and eight, but a tax or duty may be imposed on such Importation, not exceeding ten dollars for each Person.

State Power to Continue Importing Slaves

In this clause, "such Persons" refers to slaves. As soon as permitted by the Constitution, in 1808, Congress prohibited importation of slaves (though enforcement was spotty at best, impeded as it was by state officials sympathetic to the slave trade and by executives little interested in stopping it).

Clause 1.9.2 Habeas Corpus

The privilege of the Writ of Habeas Corpus shall not be suspended, unless when in Cases of Rebellion or Invasion the public Safety may require it.

Habeas Corpus

Latin for "have the body." The Constitution was written during a time when all lawyers were expected to have a working knowledge of Latin (and Greek). Nevertheless, the Constitution is notable for its *lack* of obscure Latin legalisms. The use of the term "habeas corpus" should be a clue to the term's familiarity. It named a basic right ("The Great Writ") hallowed by its antiquity in English law. It was the right to freedom from arbitrary seizure or jailing without due process. It gives prisoners the right to have their imprisonment justified before a judge.

Unless . . . Rebellion or Invasion . . . may require it

Early in the Civil War Abraham Lincoln suspended the right of habeas corpus, as did Ulysses S. Grant in battling the Ku Klux Klan.

Habeas Corpus Today

Recently, the Court has reasserted its right to review the US government's reasons for holding prisoners. The problem has been raised in the context of people, whether US citizens or not, imprisoned by the US for terrorist acts, sometimes overseas, and sometimes without trial. See *Hamdi v. Rumsfeld* (2004), *Hamdan v. Rumsfeld* (2006), and *Boumediene v. Bush* (2008).

Suspension of Habeas Corpus

The location of this clause suggests that this power belongs to Congress. But in practice, crises that may require suspension seldom lend themselves to Congress's pace. Who gets to decide when it's OK for the government to snatch whomever it wishes and put that person in jail without trial? Who decides when that period is over? This is a question to be battled out between the three branches. Congress can endorse presidential action, limit it, or bring the period of suspension to an end.

> Clause 1.9.3 Bill of Attainder, Ex Post Facto
>
> No Bill of Attainder or ex post facto Law shall be passed.

Bill of Attainder

This refers to laws that single out individuals or easily iden-
tified groups for punishment without trial. It shares a root
with the word "stain." It prohibited laws that condemned an
entire family line—see "Corruption of Blood, of Forfeiture"
under Limits on Punishment for Treason, 3.3.2.

Ex post facto Law

Again, the Latin for "after the fact" refers to a familiar legal
concept. You cannot be punished under criminal law for
acts that were legal when you did them.

> Clause 1.9.4 Capitation Tax
>
> No Capitation, or other direct, Tax shall be laid, unless in
> Proportion to the Census or Enumeration herein before
> directed to be taken.

No Capitation, or other direct, Tax . . . unless in Proportion

A capitation tax is a uniform tax on each person, or person
within a category (adult men, slaves, left-handed history
professors, etc.). This clause prevented Congress from levy-
ing a capitation tax on a type of person concentrated in a
single section of the country (Southern slaves) or, inciden-
tally, land. It was made obsolete by the 16th Amendment.

Or other direct, Tax

From debates at the Convention, it seems to refer to taxing
the *states* "directly" in a way that might burden one or more
out of proportion with their level of political representation.
(For example, a tax of $1.00 per acre of land would have
vastly more impact in North Carolina than in Connecticut.)
They were not trying to protect individuals but states. The
Court defined "direct" taxes to be only capitation/head

taxes (say, on slaves) *or* taxes on land. (When Rufus King, Constitutional Convention delegate from Massachusetts, demanded its precise meaning, "No one answd." [August 20, 1787. Max Farrand, *The Records of the Federal Convention of 1787*, 2:350]).

> Clause 1.9.5 Export Taxes on a State
>
> No Tax or Duty shall be laid on Articles exported from any State.

Export Taxes as Sectional Taxes

This is the second of three clauses, with 1.9.4 and 1.9.6, that prevent Congress from unfairly burdening one state or section to benefit the others. At the time of passage, some states exported far more than others. The Southern slave states in particular depended more on exports than on internal trade for their prosperity.

> Clause 1.9.6 State Ports
>
> No Preference shall be given by any Regulation of Commerce or Revenue to the Ports of one State over those of another: nor shall Vessels bound to, or from, one State, be obliged to enter, clear, or pay Duties in another.

Ports and Taxes

This clause prevents individual states from receiving preferential treatment from Congress. It also prevents states from taxing interstate commerce. See also Commerce Clause 1.8.3, above.

> Clause 1.9.7 Appropriations by Law Only
>
> No Money shall be drawn from the Treasury, but in Consequence of Appropriations made by Law; and a regular Statement and Account of the Receipts and Expenditures of all public Money shall be published from time to time.

No Money shall be drawn from the Treasury

This is a somewhat oddly placed clause. While it is listed under the section focused on Congress, it is most often seen as a limitation on the executive branch. The president cannot spend any money without authorization by a law. But it is also a limitation on Congress, given that it requires that expenditures go through the entire legislative process in both houses, and that accounts be published.

Shall be published from time to time

Originally the framers had required that such accounts be published annually, but they were concerned that Congress might ignore such a specific requirement if it were inconvenient in any given year.

Clause 1.9.8 Titles and Emoluments

No Title of Nobility shall be granted by the United States: And no Person holding any Office of Profit or Trust under them, shall, without the Consent of the Congress, accept of any present, Emolument, Office, or Title, of any kind whatever, from any King, Prince or foreign State.

No Title of Nobility . . . Emolument

Official titles granted by Congress implied creation of an aristocracy. If from foreign powers, such titles or offices could create divided loyalties. The now-obscure term "emolument" referred to gain of any kind, including pay or gifts. See the Foreign Gifts and Decorations Act of 1966. Although listed under Article 1, this clause has been applied to the executive branch as well.

Section 1.10 Limits on States

> Clause 1.10.1 No state shall . . .
>
> No State shall enter into any Treaty, Alliance, or Confeder-ation; grant Letters of Marque and Reprisal; coin Money; emit Bills of Credit; make any Thing but gold and silver Coin a Tender in Payment of Debts; pass any Bill of Attain-der, ex post facto Law, or Law impairing the Obligation of Contracts, or grant any Title of Nobility.

Limits on State Sovereignty

These limits on state power often overlap with the limits on Congress. The point of these clauses is to give substance to the Supremacy Clause (6.2) that made the Constitution the supreme law of the land.

Until the Court began to rule that the 14th Amendment "incorporated" some of the Bill of Rights such as freedom of speech, this was the main section of the Constitution that limited state actions. Neither did the framers, at the time they wrote this, plan on adding the Bill of Rights. They assumed most personal rights would be ensured by state governments. This section therefore listed the limits to state sovereignty that the framers thought most important to cre-ating a true national government. It also listed a few of the limits they thought most important to ensure democratic national government—such as limits on bills of attainder, ex post facto laws, breaking contracts, and noble titles.

No State shall enter into any Treaty

Only Congress can make laws regarding relations with other countries.

No State shall . . . coin Money

Only Congress may manage the money supply. This is a major difference from the Articles. Some states had deliberately inflated currency to ease debt repayment.

No State shall . . . pass any Bill of Attainder, ex post facto Law

States may pass no laws aimed at specific individuals or groups. Nor may the states punish acts that were legal when done. (Congress is also prohibited from passing such laws. See clause 1.9.3, above.)

No State shall . . . pass any . . . Law impairing . . . Contracts

Early on, the Court used this clause to protect contracts from states. See *Fletcher v. Peck* (1810) and *Dartmouth College v. Woodward* (1819). Later the Court allowed states to balance this guarantee against the public good ("police power"). For example, even if the state granted a corporate charter for selling alcohol, it could outlaw alcohol sales if it believed that doing so was good for the state. See *Boston Beer Co. v. Massachusetts* (1878). In the 1930s, the Court allowed states to relieve mortgage obligations. Much later, it created a set of rules for applying this clause. See *Home Building & Loan Association v. Blaisdell* (1934) and *Energy Reserves Group v. Kansas Power & Light* (1983).

No State shall . . . grant any Title of Nobility

Such laws granting special legal status to individuals were forbidden to both Congress and the states. See the Incompatibility and Emoluments Clause, 1.6.2.

Clause 1.10.2 Import–Export Clause

No State shall, without the Consent of the Congress, lay any Imposts or Duties on Imports or Exports, except what may be absolutely necessary for executing its inspection Laws: and the net Produce of all Duties and Imposts, laid by any State on Imports or Exports, shall be for the Use of the Treasury of the United States; and all such Laws shall be subject to the Revision and Controul of the Congress.

No State shall . . . lay any . . . Duties on Imports or Exports

The Import–Export Clause eliminated barriers to interstate trade and reinforced Congress's role as the sole source of interstate regulations. It does not exempt imported goods from state sales taxes after they have been imported and made available for sale. See the 21st Amendment, Section 2. This is also related to the Dormant Commerce Clause. See under the 21st Amendment, "Local Wineries."

Clause 1.10.3 Port Taxes and Standing Armies

No State shall, without the Consent of Congress, lay any Duty of Tonnage, keep Troops, or Ships of War in time of Peace, enter into any Agreement or Compact with another State, or with a foreign Power, or engage in War, unless actually invaded, or in such imminent Danger as will not admit of delay.

No State shall . . . lay any Duty of Tonnage

The federal government is to have sole control over management of imports and foreign policy.

No State shall . . . enter into any . . . Compact

This clause prevents states from conspiring to undermine the national government. They may make "interstate compacts" regarding basic issues such as borders and transportation.

With a foreign Power

Control over foreign policy and warfare is reserved for the federal government unless the state is invaded.

ARTICLE 2 EXECUTIVE

A strain of revolutionary thought insisted that Americans needed no single executive. The Articles of Confederation had had none. The framers' main model for such an executive position was that of the constitutional monarch of Great Britain, and they had no wish to create a new sort of king.

The framers had long experience with the theory and practice of legislatures. Their experience with executives was more with governors appointed by the British government.

One important constraint on the president that appears nowhere in the text has been self-restraint and respect for tradition. Presidents have tended to consult Congress, to obey the Supreme Court's edicts, and to follow custom.

Except when they don't. In times of crisis, presidents have focused on action over deliberation. Executive crises since Theodore Roosevelt's time have come thicker and faster. Since World War II, they seem nearly constant.

It has been an ongoing struggle: Presidents have sought to expand executive capacity to preside over a world of complexity and speed never envisioned by the framers, while Congress and the Supreme Court have sought to keep it safely bound down by checks and balances. (Congress in the past increased its staffing to keep up with the executive branch. Congress has decreased its staffing in recent years.)

The president has only a few enumerated powers:

1. Appoint judges, ambassadors, other officials.
2. Act as commander in chief of the military.
3. Make treaties.
4. Grant pardons.

All the rest are implied executive powers, and powers presidents have taken because they could.

Section 2.1 Presidential Terms and Electors

Clause 2.1.1 Executive Power and President

The executive Power shall be vested in a President of the United States of America. He shall hold his Office during the Term of four Years, and, together with the Vice President, chosen for the same Term, be elected, as follows:

The executive Power shall be vested in a President

Given the lack of enumerated restrictions for the president, some theorists argue that presidents may exercise all powers that may be defined as "executive," without limit. In practice, the president's powers, as with those of Congress and the courts, have been limited by tradition, self-restraint, and the power of the other branches.

Congressional Acquiescence

The legal doctrine of congressional acquiescence explains the limits to presidential power by the limits to what Congress can legislate and investigate. The Court has largely refused to referee between the executive and Congress unless Congress has taken clear action. See *Youngstown Sheet & Tube v. Sawyer* (1952), when the Court sided with Congress against President Harry Truman.

Congressional Limits on Executive Power

The congressional limit on executive power is largely practical. Congress struggles to deliberate in a manner sufficient to challenge modern presidents on quickly unfolding issues. Add to this the modern-day problem of massive, diffuse congressional districts and almost constant fund-raising and staff limitations. (Members typically schedule meetings on Tuesdays, Wednesdays, and Thursdays so members can travel to their districts.) In a cost-cutting move, Congress also cut its own staffing levels in the 1990s. Congress has become increasingly like a part-time board of directors facing off against a wily chief executive officer.

> Clause 2.1.2 Selecting Electors
>
> Each State shall appoint, in such Manner as the Legislature thereof may direct, a Number of Electors, equal to the whole Number of Senators and Representatives to which the State may be entitled in the Congress: but no Senator or Representative, or Person holding an Office of Trust or Profit under the United States, shall be appointed an Elector.

Each State shall appoint

State legislatures are responsible for controlling the selection of electors. This clause was a compromise. Presidents were to be elected by the people, but not directly. All electoral votes for each state go to whichever candidate wins the popular vote in that state (Maine and Nebraska split their electoral votes). While electors in some states retain the theoretical authority to vote for a candidate who did not win their state, in practice they have rarely done so. In most states, the electors are required by law to cast their votes for the candidate who wins their state.

"Faithless Electors"

What if an elector insisted on voting against his or her instructions? While this has occurred on occasion, and there is no effective law forcing electors to vote as instructed, this has never been a significant problem in an election. Tradition and self-restraint have been sufficient up to this point. In the presidential election of 2016, so-called Hamilton Electors insisted that the Electoral College ought to serve as a final check on the electoral process, as Hamilton argued it should in Federalist Paper #68.

Number of Electors

This number reflects the "Great Compromise" in which the people are represented both state-by-state (Senate) and by population (House of Representatives). Because of this, small-population states gained power over election of the president that they otherwise would not have had. Prior to the end of slavery, this rule gave voters in slave-holding states more power because slaves were counted as three-fifths of a person.

> Clause 2.1.3 Electoral College
>
> The Electors shall meet in their respective States, and vote by Ballot for two Persons, of whom one at least shall not be an Inhabitant of the same State with themselves. And they shall make a List of all the Persons voted for, and of the Number of Votes for each; which List they shall sign and certify, and transmit sealed to the Seat of the Government of the United States, directed to the President of the Senate. The President of the Senate shall, in the Presence of the Senate and House of Representatives, open all the Certificates, and the Votes shall then be counted. The Person having the greatest Number of Votes shall be the President, if such Number be a Majority of the whole Number of Electors appointed; and if there be more than

one who have such Majority, and have an equal Number of
Votes, then the House of Representatives shall immediately
chuse by Ballot one of them for President; and if no Person
have a Majority, then from the five highest on the List
the said House shall in like Manner chuse the President.
But in chusing the President, the Votes shall be taken by
States, the Representation from each State having one Vote;
A quorum for this Purpose shall consist of a Member or
Members from two thirds of the States, and a Majority
of all the States shall be necessary to a Choice. In every
Case, after the Choice of the President, the Person having
the greatest Number of Votes of the Electors shall be the
Vice President. But if there should remain two or more
who have equal Votes, the Senate shall chuse from them by
Ballot the Vice President.

Electoral College

This section has been replaced by the 12th Amendment. See
the section on the 12th Amendment to understand how the
electoral system works today.

One at least shall not be an Inhabitant of the same State with themselves

The framers were concerned that electors might vote only
for residents of their own states.

Vice President

Originally the vice president was to be the person with the
second-highest number of electoral votes. This system became outdated with the rise of political parties and with the
election of John Adams as president and his bitter political
rival and close friend Thomas Jefferson as vice president in
1796.

Clause 2.1.4 Election Day

The Congress may determine the Time of chusing the
Electors, and the Day on which they shall give their Votes;
which Day shall be the same throughout the United States.

Time of chusing the Electors

The current law requires electors to be selected on the Tues-
day after the first Monday in November.

Day on which they shall give their Votes

The current law requires each state's electors to meet, to
tabulate their votes, and send them to Washington on the
first Monday after the second Wednesday in December.

Clause 2.1.5 Eligibility to be President

No Person except a natural born Citizen, or a Citizen
of the United States, at the time of the Adoption of this
Constitution, shall be eligible to the Office of President;
neither shall any person be eligible to that Office who shall
not have attained to the Age of thirty-five Years, and been
fourteen Years a Resident within the United States.

Natural born

This has simply meant "born an American citizen." The
Court has never needed to define its precise meaning.
(Shakespeare's "of woman born" was available, had they
wished to be tricky.) The first presidents were citizens "at the
time of the Adoption."

Shall be eligible

Under the 20th Amendment, if the president-elect is
unqualified, the vice president–elect takes office until the
president-elect has qualified. This might suggest that a

president-elect who was under 35 could still be elected but not take office until his or her birthday. Any presidential hopefuls who are sufficiently impatient and will be at least, say, 33 years old by the time of the next presidential election may wish to take note.

Clause 2.1.6 Line of Succession

In Case of the Removal of the President from Office, or of his Death, Resignation, or Inability to discharge the Powers and Duties of the said Office, the Same shall devolve on the Vice President, and the Congress may by Law provide for the Case of Removal, Death, Resignation or Inability, both of the President and Vice President, declaring what Officer shall then act as President, and such Officer shall act accordingly, until the Disability be removed, or a President shall be elected.

See the 25th Amendment for a new version of this clause.

In Case of the Removal of the President

This rule of succession was not tested until 1841, when nominal Whig Party member John Tyler took over from deceased president William Henry Harrison and proceeded to upend the entire Whig platform.

In Case of . . . Inability to discharge the Powers and Duties

See the 25th Amendment, passed in 1967. The changing nature of the world creates increasing urgency to make sure that there are no gaps in executive authority.

Line of Succession

Congress has created a definite line of succession in case of the death of president and vice president at the same time. Indeed, the legal line of succession envisions the possibility of losing president, vice president, Speaker of the House, president pro tempore of the Senate, secretary of state, and successive Cabinet officers. During gatherings that bring most of the legal line of succession together, a Cabinet officer is preselected to stay away and to take over in case disaster strikes.

> Clause 2.1.7 Presidential Compensation
>
> The President shall, at stated Times, receive for his Services, a Compensation, which shall neither be increased nor diminished during the Period for which he shall have been elected, and he shall not receive within that Period any other Emolument from the United States, or any of them.

Which shall neither be increased nor diminished

Congress cannot raise or lower the president's pay during his time in office. This prevents Congress from bribing or penalizing the president. The last four words, "or any of them" refers to individual states and prevents states from bribing the president.

> Clause 2.1.8 Presidential Oath of Office
>
> Before he enter on the Execution of his Office, he shall take the following Oath or Affirmation: "I do solemnly swear (or affirm) that I will faithfully execute the Office of President of the United States, and will to the best of my Ability, preserve, protect and defend the Constitution of the United States."

Who Administers the Oath?

By tradition, the chief justice of the Supreme Court administers the oath of office. Calvin Coolidge was sworn in by his father, a notary public, in 1923. Lyndon Johnson was sworn in by Federal Judge Sarah T. Hughes after the assassination of John F. Kennedy in 1963.

Or affirm

Starting in the late 1600s, Quakers began to see oaths to tell the truth or to fulfill a promise as a suggestion that they might be untruthful in other contexts. Instead, such believers "affirmed" their truthfulness in this venue as in all others. This clause respects the distinction.

Section 2.2 Powers of the Executive

> Clause 2.2.1a Commander in Chief
>
> The President shall be Commander in Chief of the Army and Navy of the United States, and of the Militia of the several States, when called into the actual Service of the United States; he may require the Opinion, in writing, of the principal Officer in each of the executive Departments, upon any Subject relating to the Duties of their respective Offices,

Commander in Chief

National emergencies and the president's status as commander in chief of the military could put almost limitless power in the hands of an executive who desired it. Nevertheless, the US has a strong tradition of restrained executives in times of crisis and resurgent Congresses when crises ebb.

Unitary Executive

Starting in Ronald Reagan's terms of office (1980–1988), legal thinkers have argued that the president's power as commander in chief is plenary. That is, it is absolute and subject to few if any legal limitations from Congress. The Court has yet to rule definitively on this interpretation. It ultimately is a question of power among the branches of government as much as law. See "Executive Power and President," 2.1.1.

Executive Departments

The Constitution envisions advisers in a "cabinet." The term "cabinet" comes from the sense of a small room where advisers might meet. (Compare to the "bureaucrats" who work at bureaus, the French term for "desks.") Cabinet heads must be approved with the "advice and consent" of the Senate, and their departments created and funded by laws. Thus, the Constitution implies creation of an ill-defined set of executive departments partially limited by Congress.

> Clause 2.2.1b Pardons
>
> and he shall have Power to grant Reprieves and Pardons for Offenses against the United States, except in Cases of Impeachment.

Shall have Power

The power to issue pardons implies the *lesser* power to issue partial pardons or reductions in punishment, the *greater* power to do so with conditions, and the *broader* power to issue amnesty to a class. President Carter granted amnesty to an entire class of people when he pardoned Vietnam War draft resisters who fled to Canada.

Reprieves and Pardons for Offenses against the United States

A reprieve postpones punishment. A pardon ends or prevents it. Regarding human citizens the president's pardon power is plenary. The tradition by which the president pardons a turkey at Thanksgiving does not mean he can pardon all turkeys; they are privately owned and are neither persons under the 14th Amendment nor citizens.

Against the United States

Such powers apply only to federal crimes, not crimes against states or in civil lawsuits. So the president can't get

you out of a speeding ticket (state or municipal law), resolve
your divorce (civil), or change your grade in class.

Except in Cases of Impeachment

This section forbids the president from overruling an impeachment and conviction by Congress.

> Clause 2.2.2a Advice and Consent, Treaties
>
> He shall have Power, by and with the Advice and Consent
> of the Senate, to make Treaties, provided two thirds of the
> Senators present concur;

To make Treaties

Treaties require two-thirds approval from the Senate. Yet
the Supreme Court and the Senate have largely accepted
presidential control over foreign policy. Presidents interpret
treaties under their power to govern foreign policy—and
have even withdrawn treaties—without Senate advice and
consent.

> Clause 2.2.2b Appointments Clause
>
> and he shall nominate, and by and with the Advice and
> Consent of the Senate, shall appoint Ambassadors, other
> public Ministers and Consuls, Judges of the supreme
> Court, and all other Officers of the United States, whose
> Appointments are not herein otherwise provided for, and
> which shall be established by Law:

He shall nominate . . . Advice and Consent of the Senate

The president selects whom he or she wishes to appoint. But
the Senate must approve these choices.

Advice and Consent

In practice, presidents consult with the Senate to gauge
the acceptability of their choices. But the requirement that
presidents seek "Advice and Consent" applies only *after* they
choose. Presidents need gain only the "consent" of the Senate. Any useful senatorial "advice" is a bonus.

> Clause 2.2.2c Inferior Officers
>
> but the Congress may by Law vest the Appointment of
> such inferior Officers, as they think proper, in the President
> alone, in the Courts of Law, or in the Heads of Depart-
> ments.

Vest the Appointment of . . . inferior Officers

Congress (not the Senate alone) decides by law which federal officials and judges must be confirmed by Senate.

> Clause 2.2.3 Recess Appointments
>
> The President shall have Power to fill up all Vacancies that
> may happen during the Recess of the Senate, by granting
> Commissions which shall expire at the End of their next
> Session.

Power to fill up all Vacancies

Until the 1940s, Congress was out of session several months
of the year. Recess appointments were an important way
to keep the government functioning or to appoint officials to office without the advice and consent of the Senate.
When the Senate came back into session, it had the option
of confirming the official in their appointment or rejecting
them. Congress uses "pro forma" sessions, never quite going
out of session, in order to block all recess appointments.
Such actions are evidence of eroding "comity" or traditional

courtesies and respect between the branches. *National Labor Relations Board v. Noel Canning* (2014) ruled that such pro forma sessions were sufficient to prevent recess appointments by the president.

2.3 Duties of the President

Clause 2.3.1a State of the Union Report

He shall from time to time give to the Congress Information of the State of the Union, and recommend to their Consideration such Measures as he shall judge necessary and expedient;

State of the Union

The president must report to Congress "from time to time." This report was at first sent in written form to maintain separation of powers. Woodrow Wilson began the tradition of presenting it in person. The form of the State of the Union report is left undefined by the Constitution, but Congress has the power to pass specific reporting requirements into federal law regarding the executive departments.

Recommend to their Consideration such Measures

By this clause presidents gain a formal role in lawmaking. Similar to the requirement that presidents report to Congress, this role is already implied by the president's role in signing or vetoing legislation, and in enforcing it.

Clause 2.3.1b Emergency Sessions of Congress

he may, on extraordinary Occasions, convene both Houses, or either of them, and in Case of Disagreement between them, with Respect to the Time of Adjournment, he may adjourn them to such Time as he shall think proper;

Convene and Adjourn Legislature

In times of emergency, the president may call the Senate or House, or both, into a special session. No president has ever adjourned Congress under this power. See 1.5.4.

Clause 2.3.1c Receive Ambassadors
he shall receive Ambassadors and other public Ministers;

Receive Ambassadors

Neither Congress nor the states have the power to negotiate on behalf of the nation with representatives of foreign powers. This power is reserved to the president. See 2.2.2.

Clause 2.3.1d Take Care
he shall take Care that the Laws be faithfully executed,

Take Care that the Laws be faithfully executed

If "the Laws" are solely those passed by Congress, this clause requires the president to obey Congress's law. It therefore may limit more than it expands executive power. But if it means the president shall ensure lawfulness in general, then it also expands executive power. The Take Care Clause has become a way for presidents to take action to preserve domestic order in the absence of specific legislation.

Clause 2.3.1e Commission Officers
and shall Commission all the Officers of the United States.

Commission all the Officers of the United States

A president can't do all the work of taking care that the laws be faithfully executed. Therefore, presidents appoint and commission officers to carry out these duties in accordance with the Appointments Clause (2.2.2b).

Section 2.4 Impeachment of Executive

Section 2.4.1 Impeachment of Executive

The President, Vice President and all civil Officers of the United States, shall be removed from Office on Impeachment for, and Conviction of, Treason, Bribery, or other high Crimes and Misdemeanors.

Impeachment for, and Conviction of

This is a two-step process. See clauses 1.2.5 and 1.3.6 for details (see also 2.2.1b). Basically, the House of Representatives serves as a grand jury. It makes the charge. The Senate serves as the court.

Treason, Bribery . . . high Crimes and Misdemeanors

The House of Representatives has the sole power to decide what is an impeachable offense, and the Senate has the sole power to decide whether it will convict based on that charge. Two presidents, Andrew Johnson and William Jefferson Clinton have been impeached. But the Senate has never convicted a president of high crimes and misdemeanors. Richard Milhous Nixon resigned before he could be impeached.

ARTICLE 3 JUDICIAL

Alexander Hamilton declared the judicial branch the "least dangerous branch" because of its inability to make laws or execute policy. But he said so as part of the *Federalist Papers* (No. 78), and those papers were intended to sway the public in favor of ratification. The very fact that he felt compelled to dispel fears about the power of unelected judges suggests that it was an issue.

Judicial review is not explicitly mentioned in the Constitution, but it was well-established practice at the time. Still, the Court had to raise itself as the newest branch of the new national government (the Articles of Confederation included no judicial branch) to equal status with the other two branches so that each could check and balance the others.

The long-term mission of the Court has been to establish and protect its role as one of the coequal three branches of government and as final arbiter of the Constitution. Lacking the legitimating institution of direct elections, being limited mostly to an appellate role, and lacking an effective means of carrying out its decisions, it has had to achieve this goal through persuasion and precedent.

The Supreme Court adheres with almost religious fervor to decisions of previous courts—that is, to precedents, or "stare decisis." Think of the Court as semireligious interpreters of the Constitution as scripture. Their power rests on their rectitude and their links to long legal tradition. They live in constant danger of being ignored.

Section 3.1 Judicial Powers

Clause 3.1.1 Organization of the Courts

The judicial Power of the United States, shall be vested in one supreme Court, and in such inferior Courts as the Congress may from time to time ordain and establish. The Judges, both of the supreme and inferior Courts, shall hold their Offices during good Behaviour, and shall, at stated Times, receive for their Services, a Compensation, which shall not be diminished during their Continuance in Office.

And in such inferior Courts

The Constitution creates a single court, the Supreme Court. Congress has created a three-tiered system with roughly 100 federal district courts and various specialized courts for taxes, veterans appeals, international trade, and others. Above them are 13 federal appeals courts. Above them is the Supreme Court.

Marbury v. Madison, *1803*

The Court first insisted on its right to rule on the constitutionality of the laws and actions of the other branches during the first great test of the constitutional system. *Marbury v. Madison* (1803) took place during the so-called Revolution of 1800. In that year John Adams and the Federalist Party lost the election to Thomas Jefferson and his Democratic-Republicans. While the Federalists left office peacefully, they also sought to use the judicial branch to create a buffer against the new administration. Between the time they lost the election in late 1800 and the time that Jefferson was sworn in in March 1801, they added several justices of the peace and judgeships.

The winning Democratic-Republicans fought back. They passed their own laws on the number of judgeships and delayed the next term of the Supreme Court. They even held back some commissions that had been signed but not officially delivered. The men who had been named to these commissions filed suit directly to the Supreme Court under section 13 of the Judiciary Act of 1789. The court case that resulted was named after one of these men, William Marbury, and the new secretary of state, James Madison.

Marbury v. Madison put John Marshall, the newly named chief justice of the Supreme Court, in a difficult political position. The Supreme Court had yet to fully achieve a solid position under the Constitution. With the reigning Democratic-Republicans seeking every chance to undermine the judicial branch, he had little confidence that they would accept or enforce Court decisions against the executive and legislative branches.

Marshall's Court came up with a creative solution that gave
Jefferson and the Democratic-Republicans a short-term
victory but explicitly insisted on the role of the Court in
interpreting the Constitution. It ruled against Marbury
and the other Federalist "Midnight Judges" on constitutional grounds. The Court would *not* require Jefferson and
Madison to accept the appointments as provided for section
13 of the Judiciary Act. But in the Court's decision giving
Jefferson that victory, John Marshall insisted that it was
the Supreme Court's legitimate role to make such rulings
regarding the nature of the Constitution.

Marbury was not a single, magic turning point; it was
part of a historical process. In accepting his victory, it has
seemed, Jefferson also had to accept the legitimacy of the
Court's role. (Jefferson himself never conceded this point.)
Over time, the Court carved out its role as final arbiter of
the Constitution. Today the Court's judicial review powers
are far more secure.

Section 3.2 Scope of Supreme Court

Clause 3.2.1 Judicial Power (Arising)

The judicial Power shall extend to all Cases, in Law and
Equity, arising under this Constitution, the Laws of the
United States, and Treaties made, or which shall be made,
under their Authority; to all Cases affecting Ambassadors,
other public Ministers and Consuls; to all Cases of admi-
ralty and maritime Jurisdiction; to Controversies to which
the United States shall be a Party; to Controversies between
two or more States; between a State and Citizens of another
State; between Citizens of different States, between Citizens
of the same State claiming Lands under Grants of different
States, and between a State, or the Citizens thereof, and
foreign States, Citizens or Subjects.

The judicial Power shall extend

This clause is known as the "Arising Clause." The Court rules only on disagreement regarding federal functions or statutes, and only between parties with standing to bring suit.

Comparative Note

The insistence that the Court rule only within specific cases is a particularly Anglo-American model. There are many models of justice in the world. Spanish and French judges, for example, have far greater power to investigate on their own and to initiate action.

Between a State and Citizens of another State

The 11th Amendment limits the ability of citizens to sue states through the federal courts. The reason for this is to protect state sovereignty. The Court has created further limitations on the ability of Congress to create laws that allow citizens to sue their states. This is the reason that the main party with standing to bring suit against states is the federal government.

> Clause 3.2.2 Jurisdiction
>
> In all Cases affecting Ambassadors, other public Ministers and Consuls, and those in which a State shall be Party, the supreme Court shall have original Jurisdiction. In all the other Cases before mentioned, the supreme Court shall have appellate Jurisdiction, both as to Law and Fact, with such Exceptions, and under such Regulations as the Congress shall make.

Original Jurisdiction

Almost all cases come to the Court by appeal. Even in cases where the Constitution gives the Court the power to originate cases, it generally delegates that authority to specialized courts and reviews them on appeal.

> ### Clause 3.2.3 Trial by Jury
>
> The Trial of all Crimes, except in Cases of Impeachment, shall be by Jury; and such Trial shall be held in the State where the said Crimes shall have been committed; but when not committed within any State, the Trial shall be at such Place or Places as the Congress may by Law have directed.

The Trial of all Crimes . . . shall be by Jury

Trial by jury is a basic and ancient right in Anglo-American jurisprudence. See the 6th Amendment.

Section 3.3 Treason

> ### Clause 3.3.1 Defining Treason
>
> Treason against the United States, shall consist only in levying War against them, or in adhering to their Enemies, giving them Aid and Comfort. No Person shall be convicted of Treason unless on the Testimony of two Witnesses to the same overt Act, or on Confession in open Court.

Treason

What is the difference between treason and disagreeing with the government? Monarchical governments in general saw little difference. The framers insisted that the term "treason" be defined narrowly and with a high standard of proof.

> ### Clause 3.3.2 Limits on Punishment for Treason
>
> The Congress shall have Power to declare the Punishment of Treason, but no Attainder of Treason shall work Corruption of Blood, or Forfeiture except during the Life of the Person attainted.

Corruption of Blood, or Forfeiture

Under English law, a person's family and heirs could be stripped of their property and status in perpetuity ("corruption of blood"). In this way, the Constitution prohibits punishments from extending into future generations.

III.
Limitations on State Sovereignty

ARTICLE 4 STATES

Section 4.1 Each State to Honor All Others

> Clause 4.1.1 Full Faith and Credit
>
> Full Faith and Credit shall be given in each State to the public Acts, Records, and judicial Proceedings of every other State; And the Congress may by general Laws prescribe the Manner in which such Acts, Records and Proceedings shall be proved, and the Effect thereof.

Full Faith and Credit and Marriage Equality

Court judgments in one state must be honored in another. People still fly to Las Vegas, Nevada, in order to evade mandatory waiting periods and other restrictions on marriage licenses in their home states. Those quickie weddings in Las Vegas had to be honored in other states. Fear that same-sex marriages in one state would have to be honored in others led to Congress enacting a new national law, the Defense of Marriage Act (DOMA), in 1996. The portion of DOMA that permitted states to avoid giving full faith and credit to same-sex marriages was ruled unconstitutional in 2015 under the 5th Amendment's Due Process Clause. See *US v. Windsor* (2013). In 2015 the Court ruled that same-sex marriage was a 14th Amendment freedom that states were not permitted to abridge (*Obergefell v. Hodges* [2015]).

Section 4.2 Comity, or Mutual Respect

Clause 4.2.1 Privileges and Immunities

The Citizens of each State shall be entitled to all Privileges and Immunities of Citizens in the several States.

Privileges and Immunities

States may not discriminate against non-state citizens without good reason. Good reasons to discriminate include charging higher tuition for state-supported education and higher fees for hunting and fishing licenses. But students who move to a state must have a chance to "rebut the presumption" that they are temporary residents (see *Vlandis v. Kline* [1973]). Bad reasons to discriminate include reserving jobs for local residents. See the 14th Amendment for parallel language applying "privileges or immunities" of US citizens to the states.

Clause 4.2.2 Extradition Rules

A Person charged in any State with Treason, Felony, or other Crime, who shall flee from Justice, and be found in another State, shall on Demand of the executive Authority of the State from which he fled, be delivered up, to be removed to the State having Jurisdiction of the Crime.

Extradition Rules

Persons who commit a crime in one state but have moved to another state must be handed over for trial.

Clause 4.2.3 Fugitive Slave Clause

No Person held to Service or Labour in one State, under the Laws thereof, escaping into another, shall, in Consequence of any Law or Regulation therein, be discharged from such Service or Labour, but shall be delivered up

> on Claim of the Party to whom such Service or Labour
> may be due.

No Person held to Service or Labour

"No Person" refers to slaves as well as apprentices and
indentured servants. Congress enforced the clause with
the Fugitive Slave Act of 1793, although Northern states
resisted it by requiring jury trials (which often nullified or
refused to enforce the law) and by refusing to enforce it. In
Prigg v. Pennsylvania (1842), the Supreme Court upheld the
national Fugitive Slave Act and overturned Pennsylvania's
law forbidding return of slaves. Edward Prigg's conviction
under state law was therefore overturned. At the same time,
the ruling permitted states to forbid their employees from
helping to catch and return former slaves. The Compromise
of 1850 included a new Fugitive Slave Act that eliminated
juries, paid a bonus to slave catchers, required only a written assertion from the supposed former owner, and put
any black person—former slave or not—at risk of being
enslaved. This law, along with *Dred Scott* (1857) helped to
convince Northerners in the leadup to the Civil War that
slavery was becoming less of a "peculiar institution" of the
South and more of a national institution.

Section 4.3 Formation of New States

> Clause 4.3.1 Admissions Clause
>
> New States may be admitted by the Congress into this
> Union; but no new State shall be formed or erected within
> the Jurisdiction of any other State; nor any State be formed
> by the Junction of two or more States, or Parts of States,
> without the Consent of the Legislatures of the States con-
> cerned as well as of the Congress.

Without the Consent of the Legislatures

Congress can't split old states to create new states. Yet, in the Civil War, Virginia decided to secede, and the region that became West Virginia decided to secede from Virginia. Vermont, Kentucky, Tennessee, and Maine were formed from state territories with the consent of their legislatures.

Northwest Ordinance of 1787

Congress, under the Articles of Confederation, passed this law establishing the right of new states to enter the Union on an equal basis with existing states. The framers wrote the New States Clause with the Northwest Ordinance in mind.

Clause 4.3.2 Territories

The Congress shall have Power to dispose of and make all needful Rules and Regulations respecting the Territory or other Property belonging to the United States; and nothing in this Constitution shall be so construed as to Prejudice any Claims of the United States, or of any particular State.

Congress's Power in Territories of the United States

Congress has power to make laws and to rule territories. The US has controlled several "insular" territories such as Wake, Samoa, Guam, Puerto Rico, Virgin Islands, Northern Mariana Islands, and Guantanamo Bay. This designation also applies to military bases and embassies in sovereign nations and to the Green Zone in Iraq. At different times, the US has controlled the Philippines, Haiti, and other places.

Section 4.4 Republican Government

Section 4.4.1 Guarantee of a Republican Government

The United States shall guarantee to every State in this Union a Republican Form of Government, and shall protect each of them against Invasion; and on Application of the Legislature, or of the Executive (when the Legislature cannot be convened) against domestic Violence.

A Republican Form of Government

The Court has largely seen the question of defining a "Republican Form of Government" as a political question for the states and Congress to decide.

The United States shall

In this section of the Constitution "The United States" names a single nation, not a confederacy of states, united.

IV.
Ratification, Amendments, and National Supremacy

ARTICLE 5 AMENDING THE CONSTITUTION

Article 5.1 Amending the Constitution

The Congress, whenever two thirds of both Houses shall deem it necessary, shall propose Amendments to this Constitution, or, on the Application of the Legislatures of two thirds of the several States, shall call a Convention for proposing Amendments, which, in either Case, shall be valid to all Intents and Purposes, as Part of this Constitution, when ratified by the Legislatures of three fourths of the several States, or by Conventions in three fourths thereof, as the one or the other Mode of Ratification may be proposed by the Congress; Provided that no Amendment which may be made prior to the Year One thousand eight hundred and eight shall in any Manner affect the first and fourth Clauses in the Ninth Section of the first Article; and that no State, without its Consent, shall be deprived of its equal Suffrage in the Senate.

Application of the Legislatures of two thirds of the . . . States

No amendments have ever been proposed by this method.

When ratified by . . . three fourths of the several States

Only the 21st Amendment, repealing the prohibition of alcohol, was ratified by special conventions in the states.

Prohibiting Amendments to End Slavery before 1808

Slave states insisted that their constitutional right to own slaves not be amended before 1808 (see clauses 1.9.1 and 1.9.4). There was no prohibition on amendments regarding other aspects of slavery, however, such as the Fugitive Slave Clause (4.2.3) or the Three Fifths Clause (1.2.3). Nevertheless, Ben Franklin was the lead signer on an abolitionist petition to the First Congress in 1789 that challenged legislators to abolish the slave trade despite these safeguards.

ARTICLE 6 NATIONAL SUPREMACY

Clause 6.1 Continuity Clause

All Debts contracted and Engagements entered into, before the Adoption of this Constitution, shall be as valid against the United States under this Constitution, as under the Confederation.

Continuity of Obligations

This clause promises to respect obligations incurred under the previous national government. The clause reassured the nation's creditors and foreign governments.

Clause 6.2 Supremacy Clause

This Constitution, and the Laws of the United States which shall be made in Pursuance thereof; and all Treaties made, or which shall be made, under the Authority of the United States, shall be the supreme Law of the Land; and the Judges in every State shall be bound thereby, any Thing in the Constitution or Laws of any State to the Contrary notwithstanding.

Supreme Law of the Land

This is another of the places where the Constitution speaks of the nation of the United States rather than a mere federation of states, united. The Supremacy Clause made the Constitution, national laws, and treaties superior to state law. Some Anti-Federalists feared that it would reduce states to the status of administrative units.

Clause 6.3 Oaths of Office

The Senators and Representatives before mentioned, and the Members of the several State Legislatures and all executive and judicial Officers, both of the United States and of the several States, shall be bound by Oath or Affirmation, to support this Constitution; but no religious Test shall ever be required as a Qualification to any Office or public Trust under the United States.

Allegiance of State Officials to National Constitution

State officials must declare their support for the national government. Since the Constitution includes the Supremacy Clause, this oath requires that state officials owe their allegiance to the national government. See the 14th Amendment Section 3, which prohibits former officials of the Confederate States of America from serving in an official capacity again after having violated such oaths.

ARTICLE 7 RATIFICATION PROCESS

Article 7.1 Ratification

The Ratification of the Conventions of nine States, shall be sufficient for the Establishment of this Constitution between the States so ratifying the Same.

Conventions of nine States

Amendment of the Articles required unanimous consent of
all 13 states. The decision to require only nine of the 13 in
order to go into effect therefore essentially overturned the
previous Constitution's provisions for amendment. In that
sense, it overturned the previous form of government and
provided the means of creating a new one.

Between the States so ratifying the Same

The Constitution by its own authority became law as of
June 21, 1788, when New Hampshire ratified it by a 57–47
vote. By a similarly narrow vote, Virginia ratified it on June 25,
1788. But the states of New York (July 26, 1788), North Carolina (November 21, 1789), and Rhode Island (May 29, 1790)
remained nominally outside the US until they ratified.

Unanimous Consent of the States present

Done in Convention by the Unanimous Consent of the
States present the Seventeenth Day of September in the
Year of our Lord one thousand seven hundred and Eighty
seven and of the Independence of the United States the
Twelfth. In witness of whereof We have hereunto sub-
scribed our Names,

G°. Washington—Presid^t. and deputy from Virginia

Delaware
  Geo. Read
  Gunning Bedford Jun.
  John Dickinson
  Richard Bassett
  Jaco. Broom
Maryland
  James McHenry
  Daniel of St. Thos. Jenifer
  Danl Carroll

Virginia
  John Blair
  James Madison Jr.

North Carolina
  Wm Blount
  Richd Dobbs Spaight
  Hu Williamson

South Carolina
  J. Rutledge

Charles Cotesworth
  Pinckney
Charles Pinckney
Pierce Butler

Georgia
  William Few
  Abr. Baldwin

New Hampshire
  John Langdon
  Nicholas Gilman

Massachusetts
  Nathaniel Gorham
  Rufus King

Connecticut
  Wm Saml Johnson
  Roger Sherman

New York
  Alexander Hamilton

New Jersey
  Wil. Livingston
  David Brearly
  Wm Paterson
  Jona. Dayton

Pennsylvania
  B. Franklin
  Thomas Mifflin
  Robt Morris
  Geo. Clymer
  Thos Fitzsimons
  Jared Ingersoll
  James Wilson
  Gouv. Morris

Attest: William Jackson, *Secretary*

Unanimous Consent of the States present

At the very moment when the Constitutional Convention
completed its arguments and debates, they faced a problem.
Not all of the participants in the convention fully sup-
ported the text. Not all states were present. This formulation
"Unanimous Consent of the States present" cleverly masked
the lingering dissent. Elbridge Gerry of Massachusetts
refused to sign the Constitution because it lacked a Bill of
Rights. George Mason, so active in the convention itself,
refused to sign the Constitution because it lacked the Bill of
Rights and for broader reasons. New York's representatives
had all left except for Alexander Hamilton. Rhode Island
refused to send delegates.

It was at this moment that Benjamin Franklin wrote, and had James Wilson read, the speech quoted on this book's opening pages. Franklin did not speak to the genius of the Constitution or its timeless perfection. He described it as a necessity and as the best that could be achieved at that moment.

V.
Amendments

BILL OF RIGHTS

The first ten amendments to the Constitution are known as the "Bill of Rights." The Bill mostly lists individual rights the federal government is bound to respect. The 14th Amendment (1868) seemed to promise transformation of the Bill into a list of rights owed all Americans by all levels of government, including states.

Why Did the Framers Leave the Bill Out?

The Constitution originally had no Bill of Rights. Opponents pointed to the missing Bill as evidence of a power grab. The framers claimed that they had omitted the Bill because there was no need for one; the federal government had no ability to do anything (such as abridge freedom of speech) that went unnamed. Moreover, to name a specific list of rights would be to suggest they were the *only* rights that the new national government was bound to respect. (The 9th Amendment addressed this issue.)

But proponents of the Constitution soon agreed that the first Congress would put forward such a Bill as a condition of passage. James Madison, originally an opponent of such a Bill, saw it as a chance to give the federal government veto power over state laws. His amendment giving Congress this power failed to make the final list, however.

The Bill of Rights as Limit on the Powers of Congress Only

In *Barron v. Baltimore* (1833) the Court ruled that the Bill of Rights applied to the national government, not the states.

Bill of Rights as Human Rights

Some observers before and after the Supreme Court established the precedent in *Barron v. Baltimore* nevertheless have insisted on seeing the rights in the Bill as basic guarantees of individual rights under natural and common law against all levels of government, be they national, state, or local. That is, they see the Bill as "declaratory" of American rights under ancient tradition. Legally, they were wrong; by 1833, the Court had explicitly ruled so. Rhetorically, the argument had power; not everyone read Supreme Court rulings.

Starting in the twentieth century, the idea that the Bill of Rights listed basic human rights that all government agencies must respect has gained more legal power, and Americans routinely list the Constitution's Bill of Rights as a sacred, absolute, and inviolable list of human rights, almost a "Ten Commandments" for the government.

The Twentieth-Century Rights Revolution

Protecting basic rights became more complex as more Americans began to demand them. Rights were simpler when largely the special possession of white men who held a measure of social status and economic independence. The framers tempered democracy with the unspoken assumption that a meritocracy of white male elites would rule, and that equality and rights would be handed out on a sliding scale.

But increasing numbers of Americans soon clamored for inclusion. Many poor white men made this claim at the dawn of the two-party political system circa 1800. Many more made this claim when mass political parties developed in the Jacksonian era (named after President Andrew Jackson) of the 1830s. Immigrant groups such as Germans, Irish, and Italians in time claimed their due.

After the Civil War, black male Americans successfully made a claim for political rights. With the failure of Reconstruction, however, Southern blacks largely lost the vote. (Women attempted to claim political rights in this era, too, but without even the temporary success of black men.) In his less-famous response to Abigail Adams's request that he "Remember the ladies," John Adams predicted such a deluge. If protections were granted to women, he noted, there would soon be no reason to exclude anyone at all from equality.

The twentieth century has seen Adams's prediction come true. There has been an explosion of groups claiming equal treatment under the law, including women. Children, too, have gained additional access to civil rights, including the right to education and health care. The civil rights movement cracked open politics for African Americans a hundred years after the Civil War. Hispanics and Indians made similar claims. That crack has proved wide enough for additional groupings, including those based in gender and sexuality. The main groups whose equality the government seems able to evade today include political radicals, the very poor, new immigrants (especially illegal immigrants), and people—especially teenagers—who live in specific areas, whom the police have come to suspect as a class, and who have little political power.

Most defendants with court-appointed lawyers tend to settle for negotiated sentences rather than exercising their right for a trial by a jury of their peers. Wealth and celebrity bring de facto additional protections, including increased procedural protections and energetic legal representation.

The Transformative Impact of the 14th Amendment

Starting in 1873, the Court insisted that the 14th Amendment had made little change in the meaning of the Bill of Rights. Late in the nineteenth century, however, the Court decided that it *did* create a new national right for all Americans but that it mostly protected *economic* liberty. In the "laissez faire" era (roughly 1880s–1937), the Court prohibited almost *all* state economic regulations as infringements on "liberty of contract." (At the same time, it construed the Commerce Clause power of Congress narrowly to prohibit most national economic regulation.) Only in 1938 did it begin to slowly rediscover the civil rights guarantees of the 14th Amendment. See the discussion of the 14th Amendment for more on liberty of contract and other issues mentioned here.

Progressive Challenge to Laissez Faire

Around 1900, some Americans began to argue that this new era of large-scale corporate power demanded government regulations to guarantee individual freedoms. Progressives argued that not only abuse of public governmental power (as envisioned by the Constitution) but also private accumulations of power could produce tyranny. Maximum individual liberty, Progressives insisted, required government limitations on private economic power.

Civil Rights: A New Balance Point

The Court pulled back from protecting absolute property rights and, during the Great Depression, from forbidding most economic legislation. It indicated in a footnote that it would begin to protect civil rights for politically vulnerable groups (See footnote 4 in *US v. Carolene Products* [1938]).

Incorporation of the Bill of Rights through the 14th Amendment

The process of defining civil liberties protected by the 14th Amendment in terms of the rights listed in the Bill is known as "incorporation." This means that the rights listed under the Bill should be considered basic liberties under the 14th Amendment (and therefore ought to be "incorporated" into its protections). Justice Hugo Black insisted that unless there was 100 percent incorporation, the justices would simply be substituting their own judgment for that of state legislatures. Yet it has not been clear to a majority of justices that the 14th Amendment ought to be so broad as to include such a blanket new limit on state sovereignty. Nor has the Court been willing to make such a massive change all at once. It has, more cautiously, practiced "selective incorporation," gradually ruling which rights ought to be incorporated as basic liberties and which should not.

Starting in *Chicago, Burlington & Quincy Railroad Co. v. City of Chicago* (1897) the Court effectively incorporated the 5th Amendment "Takings Clause," which prohibits the government from taking private property without due process and due compensation. It began to apply the "Due Process" Clause of the 14th Amendment to state legal proceedings in *Twining v. New Jersey* (1908). It was not until *Gitlow v. New York* (1925), however, that the Court began to explicitly list liberties so fundamental that they would henceforth be incorporated through the 14th Amendment's Due Process Clause. *Gitlow* incorporated the 1st Amendment freedom of speech and press.

See specific amendments for their incorporation status.

The first ten amendments (the Bill of Rights) were ratified effective December 15, 1791.

1st Amendment—Freedom of Speech, Press, Assembly, Religion, Petition

Congress shall make no law respecting an establishment of religion, or prohibiting the free exercise thereof; or abridging the freedom of speech, or of the press, or the right of the people peaceably to assemble, and to petition the Government for a redress of grievances.

1st Amendment Outline

1. Establishment Clause
   a. Separation of Church and State
   b. Lemon Test
2. Freedom of Speech
   a. Flag Burning
   b. Libel and Parody
   c. Commercial Speech
   d. Political Speech
   e. Obscenity and Pornography
3. Freedom of the Press
4. Peaceably to Assemble
5. Petition the Government
6. Incorporation of the 1st Amendment
7. Student Free Speech
8. Peter Zenger: Pre-Constitutional Precedent

1. Establishment Clause

   Controversy was caused by the 1st Amendment's incorporation of the Establishment Clause through the 14th Amendment in *Everson v. Board of Education* (1947) (see below, under "6. Incorporation of the 1st Amendment"). The Establishment Clause was hardly an issue for much of our history. But states and municipalities had long regulated religion and morality. This new rule forbidding such regulations thus undermined long-standing community arrangements.

For example, it made legally required Christmas pageants and recital of the Lord's Prayer more difficult to sustain as neutral exercises of government power. Previously, parents and children of non-Protestant faiths had simply adapted to these facts of life, "hmmm hmm-ing" key words to religious songs, enrolling in private schools, or (in at least one high school drama club) insisting that all actors in a state-mandated school Christmas pageant be Jewish "for reasons of historical accuracy."

a. Separation of Church and State

The original reasons for separating church and state came from a desire to keep the church free from government corruption. This was Roger Williams's reason for attacking Puritan theocracy in the 1630s. Today religious activists seem more interested in using religion to purify government—to bring back old community limits on moral behavior.

b. Lemon Test

In *Lemon v. Kurtzman* (1971) the Court created three tests to decide whether state actions violated the Establishment Clause. Laws must have a nonreligious purpose, tend neither to help nor to hurt religion, and not excessively entangle government and religion. If a law did any of these three things, it was unconstitutional. See *Kitzmiller v. Dover Area School District* (2005).

The problem of Court rulings on the Establishment Clause came from the doctrine that Court rulings apply universally, coherently, and consistently. Once the Court decided to rule on separation of church and state, it stepped into the bewildering complexity and variety of community rules, customs, moral norms, and religions. Once it decided that government had to be kept out of the business of policing religion, it came into conflict with already established local governmental practices entwined with religion.

Free exercise thereof

The Court applied the "strict scrutiny" test developed for civil rights cases against government regulation of religious practices starting with *Sherbert v. Verner* (1963). In this test, the government had to show a "compelling interest" in regulating a religious practice. In the 1980s and 1990s, the Court authorized more government regulations. In *City of Boerne v. Flores* (1997), the Court ruled that Boerne had the right to impose zoning ordinances on a church without violating the Free Exercise Clause. That is, Boerne did not have to show a "compelling interest," because its zoning ordinances were neutral regarding religion.

2. Freedom of Speech

   The first-ever ruling on freedom of speech came in *Schenck v. US* (1919) and in the context of World War I. Eugene Debs went to prison for encouraging resistance to the draft in World War I (*Debs v. US* [1919]). Thousands were convicted of criticizing the war effort or obstructing the draft. (Prior to 1919, guarantees of free speech were largely dormant. The Alien and Sedition Acts of 1798, passed in order to prevent criticism of Federalists, were allowed to expire in 1801.)

   Most people remember *Schenk* for Justice Oliver Wendell Holmes Jr.'s comparison of actively opposing war during wartime to yelling fire in a crowded theater. He actually likened it to *falsely* yelling fire in a crowded theater. Holmes himself quickly abandoned this metaphor, so much more vivid than helpful. (What, he was asked, if the theater actually *was* on fire?) Yet, even without Holmes's support, his original reasoning helped establish broad limits on free speech among a majority of justices. (In a dissent later in the year [*Abrams v. US* (1919)], Holmes sought to narrow the definition of "clear and present danger" more to acts rather than to speech.)

Nevertheless, in *Gitlow v. New York* (1925) the Court confirmed its original view of the "clear and present danger" test. At the same time, it broke new ground, stating that freedom of speech that was *not* a clear and present danger would now be considered a core liberty under the 14th Amendment. (See "6. Incorporation of the 1st Amendment.") The Court expanded protection of speech that advocated violence and resistance to the law in *Yates v. US* (1957). In *Brandenburg v. Ohio* (1969), it established a new, stricter test for when speech became illegal: "imminent, lawless action." (This result overturned the conviction of an Ohio Ku Klux Klan leader for threats against blacks and Jews.)

a. Flag Burning

In *Texas v. Johnson* (1989) the Court ruled that burning the flag was a legitimate exercise of free speech.

b. Libel and Parody

In the early 1960s, as the press began to write about resistance to civil rights, some Southern public officials responded to the criticism with libel suits against Northern newspapers. The Court issued a ruling in *New York Times Co. v. Sullivan* (1964) that raised a high bar for such suits. They had to show more than factual errors to prove libel, the Court ruled. For a public individual to sue the press for libel, he or she would have to show that the press knowingly acted with "actual malice," or with deliberate recklessness or maliciousness. *Hustler Magazine v. Falwell* (1988) protected parody and satire. Note: Parody and satire are protected even if the subject doesn't find it funny.

c. Commercial Speech

Prior to 1976, rules prohibited lawyers and doctors from advertising. So-called ambulance chasers (personal injury lawyers) had to actually *chase* the ambulances to sign up injured clients. They couldn't just put up billboards along the likely route to the hospital, and couldn't air TV commercials. Nor were drug companies allowed to advertise prescription drugs. Now they can. See *Bates v. State Bar of Arizona* (1977), *Greater New Orleans Broadcasting Association v. US* (1999), and *Thompson v. Western States Medical Center* (2002).

d. Political Speech

The Court uses "strict scrutiny" to judge the constitutionality of state or federal laws limiting political speech. It has been particularly suspicious of laws that limit spending on political campaigns. The Court has permitted campaign finance laws that require disclosure of contributions and that limit individual contributions to campaigns (*Buckley v. Valeo* [1976]). But it insisted that individual persons should be able to spend as much of their own funds as they wished on their own campaigns. In 2010 the Court struck down limits on the right of corporations to pay for commercials or videos on political themes during federal campaigns. See *Citizens United v. Federal Election Commission* (2010).

e. Obscenity and Pornography

Outside of child pornography, the Court has steadily made it harder to censor speech. The "Roth Rule" from *Roth v. US* (1957) outlawed pornography that violated community norms by appealing mostly to "prurient interests." It assumed a community. Pornography also had to come into the community in order to be obscene (not simply be stashed in a drawer; see *Stanley v. Georgia* [1969]). Neither the Court nor Congress has found a consistent test to define adult pornography without appeal to community standards. Justice Potter Stewart's declaration that "I know it when I see it" (*Jacobellis v. Ohio* [1964]) did not suggest a wish to review potential subjects himself. Rather, it indicated the difficulty of stating a consistent rule.

In 1973 the Court acknowledged the limits of the Roth rule by creating a three-part test to evaluate whether a work could be protected as free speech under the 1st Amendment. The first part echoed the Roth rule in relying on the judgment of an average person in that community. Would an average person judge that it appealed primarily to prurient interests? The second part asks if the work depicts acts forbidden under state law. The third part asks whether the work has literary, artistic, political, or scientific value. If an average person in the community would see it as chiefly prurient, and if it is forbidden by state law, and if it lacks literary, artistic, political, or scientific value, it can be banned (*Miller v. California* [1973]).

3. Freedom of the Press

    Main issues of freedom of the press include "prior restraint" (prevention of publication), the press's right of access to government meetings, and postpublication prosecution for libel or breach of national security. (In today's age of internet-based publication, the distinction between freedom of speech and freedom of the press has blurred.)

4. Peaceably to Assemble

    The right to assemble in support of such *awful* political causes as racism and anti-Semitism is protected along with the right of people to assemble in support of such *good* causes as tolerance (see *Village of Skokie v. National Socialist Party of America* [1977]). The 1st Amendment protects minority positions, even awful ones. Since the 1960s, the Court has largely refused to define or to recognize adjectives such as "awful" or "good" as related to political causes or speech.

5. Petition the Government

    The government has less scope to regulate political speech
    in traditionally public areas such as parks. But it may
    make content-neutral regulations as to the time, place,
    and manner of protests. Recently, police and the Secret
    Service have more aggressively used "free speech zones"
    to remove protesters from places near politically charged
    events such as presidential speeches. This has become
    more widespread after disruption of the World Trade
    Association meeting in 1999.

6. Incorporation of the 1st Amendment

    The Court incorporated the freedom of the press to pub-
    lish without prior restraint by the states as guaranteed by
    the 14th Amendment in *Near v. Minnesota* (1931). State
    and federal governments were allowed prior restraint only
    in cases of urgent national security (such as publishing
    shipping schedules during wartime) or obscenity. Indi-
    viduals damaged by false and malicious publications could
    sue for damages after the fact, but they could not prevent
    publication.

    The Pentagon Papers

    In *New York Times Co. v. US* (1971), the "Pentagon
    Papers" case, the US attempted to get a court order
    preventing prior publication of secret reports on national
    security grounds (as if the contents were equivalent to
    shipping schedules during wartime). The Court refused
    to so order.

7. Student Free Speech

    Students gained free speech during the 1960s era of civil
    rights and anti–Vietnam War protests (see *Tinker v. Des
    Moines. . .* [1969]). This, however, was for symbolic speech
    (black armbands). More recently, public school students
    have been punished for advocating drug use or other
    causes argued to be disruptive to education or student

privacy. See *Bethel School District No. 403 v. Fraser* (1986), *Morse v. Frederick* (2007), and *Hazelwood School District v. Kuhlmeier* (1988).

8. Peter Zenger: Pre-Constitutional Precedent

In this 1735 case, the jury disregarded the judge and decided the law itself was wrong. This precedent precedes the United States, and therefore it precedes the 1st Amendment. Nevertheless, it serves as part of American legal custom. Note, too, that the jury nullified the law, ignoring instructions from the judge. (See "Jury: Nullification," under the 6th Amendment, below.)

2nd Amendment—Right to Keep and Bear Arms

A well regulated Militia, being necessary to the security of a free State, the right of the people to keep and bear Arms, shall not be infringed.

Well regulated

For "well regulated," think "well-organized." Think, "well-connected to a legitimate, established political entity" (such as a town or community).

Militia

Being part of a "militia" or "training band" in colonial America was as much a duty as a right. Law-abiding male citizens in a town were *required* to maintain functioning firearms, to attend training days, and to serve in the militia. If they failed to do so, they were subject to penalties. They elected officers and served with neighbors. Militia defended each town. In the Revolution, militia fought with the Continental Army and defended against British Loyalists.

The militia was not quite the equivalent of today's National Guard (The National Guard is closer to the sort of standing

army that the militia was supposed to be a check against).
It's perhaps closer to a volunteer fire department today in
the mix of informal voluntarism and formal community
and government support.

The people

The "militia" and "people" were largely synonymous in
this context. They were not "the individuals" but the same
"people" in "We the People" in the Preamble.

Keep and bear Arms

This is the right—and obligation—of individuals to own
(keep) weapons and to carry (bear) them in their militia.

Shall not be infringed

The right to keep and bear military-style arms has long been
infringed by community standards and state law. (The 2nd
Amendment originally limited *national* law only.) Infringement by federal law is more recent. The National Firearms
Act was passed in 1934, largely in response to the rise of
organized crime during Prohibition, and largely in order to
regulate the supposed weapons of organized crime: sawed-
off shotguns, machine guns, grenades, and the like. Using
the Commerce Clause as its authority, the National Firearms Act imposed a prohibitive tax on the interstate sale or
transfer of such weapons. In a limited ruling in *US v. Miller*
(1939), the Court upheld the law. The law has been amended
and reaffirmed by Congress several times since 1939.

Impact of the Civil War and the 14th Amendment

Akhil Reed Amar's book *The Bill of Rights: Creation and Reconstruction* captures a sense in which the emphasis of the
2nd Amendment shifted between 1789 and 1868. He writes:
"In Reconstruction a new vision was aborning: when guns

were outlawed, only the Klan would have guns" (266). The importance of the 2nd Amendment for Northern reformers had become more about individual defense against "private violence and the lapses of local government" rather than about collective local defense against a tyrannical national army.

US v. Miller *(1939)*

The Court upheld the right of the national government to regulate interstate commerce of firearms. The Court's reasoning was in part based on the supposed inappropriateness of a sawed-off shotgun, the type of weapon that was seized in this case, for militia use. Although the Court has recently begun to veer from some of the logic of the *Miller* ruling as it pertains to interpretation of the militia clause, it has let stand the National Firearms Act's effective limits on more destructive, military-style weapons—such as sawed-off shotguns.

One might well argue that the militia clause ought to *particularly* prevent infringement of the right to own military-style weapons. But discouraging private ownership of machine guns, howitzers, missiles of various kinds, modern fighter jets, grenades, and atomic bombs have been commonly accepted as reasonable limits on 2nd Amendment rights. *Miller* limited the right to bear arms to those small weapons that a citizen (and therefore a potential militia member) might commonly be expected to keep at home (acceptable weapons include rifles, standard shotguns, and handguns).

Presser v. Illinois *(1886)*

Presser v. Illinois allowed states to forbid private militias. The right to bear arms, the Court argued, was an individual right. The right to regulate militias was a state function. The

2nd Amendment limited the national government, not the
states.

Dred Scott v. Sandford *(1857)*

Dred Scott v. Sandford suggested that *if* the slave Dred Scott
were free and white, he would be protected by the 2nd
Amendment in his individual right to bear arms.

US v. Cruikshank *(1875)*

US v. Cruikshank prevented the national government from
guaranteeing the right of individuals—in this case, black
freedmen who had armed themselves to defend against the
Ku Klux Klan—to bear arms. This was solely a state function. (A state function, it should be noted, that Southern
states had no intention of fulfilling. The Klan would now
deprive black citizens of their rights without fear of interference from the national government.)

Today's 2nd Amendment

Today's 2nd Amendment has focused on the right of
individuals to possess firearms for *private* use. That is, for
target-shooting, hunting, and individual self-defense. The
2nd Amendment's guarantee of a collective right to organize
a well-regulated militia in resistance against a potentially
tyrannical government has faded in the Court's reasoning.
This notion nevertheless retains something of a hold in
informal constitutionalism if not in current legal precedent.

Individual Right to Keep Arms

In *DC v. Heller* (2008), the Court overruled a Washington,
DC, law banning all handguns and requiring that other
weapons be stored in a manner that would prevent their
rapid use for self-defense. A total ban on handguns was
ruled unconstitutional under the 2nd Amendment. Most

recently, in *McDonald v. Chicago* (2010) the Court seems to have incorporated the right to bear arms in self-defense under the 14th Amendment's guarantee of liberties.

Note: The Court has upheld laws limiting gun ownership by the mentally incompetent and by felons.

3rd Amendment—Quartering Troops

> No Soldier shall, in time of peace be quartered in any house, without the consent of the Owner, nor in time of war, but in a manner to be prescribed by law.

This largely obsolete amendment referred to a grievance listed in the Declaration of Independence. It may be seen, in concert with the 2nd Amendment, as a guard against standing armies. It is also cited in scattered cases and in finding a right to privacy in *Griswold v. Connecticut* (1965).

4th Amendment—Unreasonable Search and Seizure

> The right of the people to be secure in their persons, houses, papers, and effects, against unreasonable searches and seizures, shall not be violated, and no Warrants shall issue, but upon probable cause, supported by Oath or affirmation, and particularly describing the place to be searched, and the persons or things to be seized.

The 4th Amendment limits when government officials may come into your house, harass you anywhere else, and frisk, poke around, arrest, trespass, or otherwise violate your wish to be left alone. It has two main parts.

The first part has come to mean: The government may violate this right as long as it does so in a manner and for reasons that the Court sees as "reasonable."

The second part explains what it means by "reasonable": A representative of the judicial branch may authorize a

representative of the executive branch to search and seize
specific places and specific persons for specific reasons stated
under oath. Those reasons must show "probable cause"
to believe criminal activity is taking place. Searches and
seizures made without a warrant are generally assumed to be
unreasonable.

Warrantless Searches or Seizures

Can the government arrest, question, search, seize, or detain
you without getting a warrant? Probably. Rules on the 4th
Amendment are complex and technical. In sum: The Court
generally privileges the government's duty to keep society
secure over your 4th Amendment rights to be left alone.

History: A Man's House Is His Castle

The most famous declaration of the English freedom from
arbitrary searches is William Pitt's declaration in Parliament, 1763: "The poorest man may in his cottage, bid
defiance to all the forces of the Crown. It may be frail, its
roof may shake; the wind may blow through it; the storm
may enter; the rain may enter; but the King of England cannot enter; all his force dares not cross the threshold of the
ruined tenement." Pitt lost. The intrusive tax law passed.

Pitt did not originate this so-called Castle Doctrine. The
term came from British Common Law champion Edward
Coke in *Semayne's Case* (1604). At what point can an officer
of the law enter a privately owned house or garden? (The
term "garden" originally referred to enclosed property.)
Coke claimed that the king's officers needed a warrant in
order to enter a private home, and if they did not announce
their purpose before breaking in, the homeowner had a
right to resist their entry.

John Adams claimed that the Revolution was born in
defense of the Castle Doctrine, in resistance to the right of
British tax collectors to enter and seize property without

specific warrants. Adams and others were particularly angry about Navigation Acts, which gave British customs officials almost unlimited power to search property. Adams was in the audience when American lawyer James Otis echoed Coke's 1604 Castle Doctrine in the "Writs of Assistance" or "Paxton's Case" (1761). British customs officials, Otis insisted, were forbidden to search private property without a specific warrant. It should be noted that, like Semayne and Pitt, Otis *lost*. Any search authorized by the king was accepted as legitimate under English courts.

Otis and Pitt based their reasoning on Coke's Common Law argument regarding scope of the Magna Carta of 1215. The 4th Amendment was a direct response to this dispute. (More recently, debate over Castle Doctrine has focused on "stand your ground" statutes, but these statutes have a glancing relationship at most to the 4th Amendment.)

Unreasonable searches and seizures

Abolitionists looked in vain to the 4th Amendment's guarantee of freedom to void the Fugitive Slave Act. Although they claimed that it ought to protect free blacks from warrantless seizure under the Fugitive Slave Act, the Court decided in *Jones v. Van Zandt* (1847) that this was essentially a political question for state and federal authorities to battle out on their own.

Incorporation

In *Mapp v. Ohio* (1961), the Court incorporated parts of the 4th Amendment as one of the 14th Amendment's "due process" liberties. It thereby began to develop and apply uniform rules across the entire nation.

Exclusionary Rule

What if the FBI ignored the 4th Amendment, broke down your door, and found evidence of a crime? From *Weeks v.*

US (1914) to *US v. Leon* (1984), the Court required that
such evidence be automatically excluded from your trial.
They reasoned that without such a rule, federal officers
would have little incentive to respect 4th Amendment
limitations. Between 1914 and 1961, the Exclusionary Rule
remained applicable only to federal cases and to states that
chose to adopt it.

Chipping Away at the Exclusionary Rule

Despite the importance of this rule in forcing police to
professionalize, it galled prosecutors and judges, seeming
to protect criminal activity more than a basic respect for
privacy. The Court increasingly weakened this aspect of the
4th Amendment even as it insisted that the right to privacy
was a basic liberty. (See the desire to reject *Weeks* in the
majority opinion in *Wolf v. Colorado* [1949]).

Objective Good Faith

The Court has relaxed its strict Exclusionary Rule to the
extent that it has been able to argue that so doing will not
encourage police illegality. It has decided that if police find
evidence of wrongdoing even with a flawed warrant it is
admissible (*US v. Leon* [1984]).

Prohibition Era: Automobiles

In the Prohibition era (1920–1933), the federal government
expanded its law enforcement efforts. In particular, federal
agents began tapping telephones and searching cars. The
Court refused to rule eavesdropping a violation of the 4th
Amendment, even when it involved wiretapping or other
electronically enhanced efforts (*Olmstead v. US* [1928]). It
reversed itself in *Katz v. US* (1967). In *Carroll v. US* (1925),
the Court ruled that 4th Amendment prohibitions may be
relaxed when searching automobiles for alcohol. The Court

has continued to give the police greater latitude to search automobiles than homes.

5th Amendment—Due Process, Property

No person shall be held to answer for a capital, or otherwise infamous crime, unless on a presentment or indictment of a Grand Jury, except in cases arising in the land or naval forces, or in the Militia, when in actual service in time of War or public danger; nor shall any person be subject for the same offense to be twice put in jeopardy of life or limb, nor shall be compelled in any criminal case to be a witness against himself, nor be deprived of life, liberty, or property, without due process of law; nor shall private property be taken for public use without just compensation.

Summary

This amendment stops the federal government from prosecuting individuals for arbitrary or political reasons, and from doing so in an unfair manner. The limitations on the government's power to prosecute have been incorporated by the Due Process Clause of the 14th Amendment. Thus, they are applicable in state and local law as well.

No person

These rights apply to all *persons* under the jurisdiction of the United States, not only citizens.

Grand Jury

The government cannot simply order that a person be put to trial. A group of ordinary citizens must agree that the trial is warranted. This ancient right was originally conceived as a guarantee against arbitrary arrest and trial. In modern times, the grand jury has become less of a guarantee against arbitrary prosecution and more of a means of gathering evidence before trial. Grand juries, because they are not prosecuting crimes, have far more leeway for compelling testimony.

Grand Jury Incorporation

The Court has not seen the 5th Amendment guarantee of a grand jury as fundamental under the 14th Amendment. Therefore, it is not binding on the states. About half of all states require grand juries for serious crimes.

Twice in jeopardy

Criminal trials are awful, damaging ordeals for defendants. The government must be prevented from using repeated trials themselves as punishment. In actual practice, the right to not be charged twice for the same crime ("double jeopardy") is complicated by technical questions, mostly revolving around three questions: When does a trial truly begin? What is the same crime? What is the same punishment?

Compelled . . . to be a witness against himself

No one can be forced to incriminate themselves. This hard-won right is rooted deep in British and American history. Here is the logic: The government, with its monopoly on coercion, must build the case on its own. It cannot demand that you build a case against yourself.

When Is a Confession Truly Voluntary?

The Court largely stayed out of the business of settling matters of voluntary confessions until recently. After all, its job was to set rules of interpretation, not to peek over the shoulders of police detectives in grubby interrogation rooms. It left details of law enforcement to communities. Only the most brutal of abuses compelled the Court to intervene. In *Brown v. Mississippi* (1936) three black men were publicly tortured until they confessed, and the torture was part of

the official evidence of the case. This case takes us back
to the origins of the right against forced self-confessions
in ancient British precedent, when the king's prosecutors
compelled confessions or pleas through torture.

Miranda Rules

Once the Court weighed in on what constituted a voluntary
versus a compelled confession, they found themselves on
slippery ground. The Court took 30 years from *Brown* in
1936 to the so-called Miranda rules (from the name of the
case *Miranda v. Arizona* [1966]) to settle the issue.

Miranda rules insist on specific, legalistic grounds on which
criminal defendants can be questioned. First, defendants
must be informed of their rights. Second, once they asked
for their 6th Amendment right to counsel, *all* questioning
must stop. The so-easily caricatured ("You have the right
to *shut up!*") ritual of Mirandizing suspects responds to a
world in which the police at times abuse their awesome
power to detain, isolate, and intimidate, particularly against
vulnerable groups with limited access to political power.

Limiting Miranda

The first Miranda era excluded any self-incriminatory
testimony that seemed to have been compelled *in any way
whatsoever*. The Court seemed to assume confessions in
the context of an arrest were suspect. Proof of a compelled
confession could "taint" any subsequent prosecution and
require the entire case to be thrown out, no matter how
strong the rest of the evidence.

Without directly overruling *Miranda*, the Court has
steadily moved away from its requirements. In *Arizona v.
Fulminante* (1991) the Court ruled that a coerced confession could be thrown out without tainting the rest of the
evidence in the case. The Court has allowed police more
leeway as they have seemed to become more restrained,

professional guardians of law—and as the egregious abuses
of earlier eras fade from memory.

Due process of law

The original meaning of this term focuses on fair procedures. The government is granted the massive power of de-
priving a person life, liberty, and property only if it follows
fair and consistent rules tested by long usage.

Substantive Due Process

The Court first used this reasoning regarding the right of
slaveholders to their human property in the infamous *Dred
Scott v. Sandford* decision (1857). The substance of the right
to property, the Court argued, was so important that there
existed no due process by which Congress could take such
property (slaves) from their owners. Therefore, it ruled,
congressional limits on ownership of slaves were unconstitutional. Congress wrote the 14th Amendment in part to
overrule this decision.

See the 14th Amendment for discussion of the Court's
Gilded Age (1870–1900) revival of substantive due process.
Here again the Court deemed property rights to be so
important as to prohibit states from regulating almost any
aspect of economic activities.

Abolitionist Argument

Abolitionists argued that since slaves were persons, they
could not be deprived of life or liberty under this clause. If
there were any such thing as substantive due process, they
argued, it should free all slaves.

Nor shall private property be taken

Given the various interpretations of the Court, this "takings
clause" might as well read: "The government has the right to

use your property as long as it can connect it to a reasonable public purpose. It probably has to reimburse you." See *Kelo v. City of New London* (2005). Post *Kelo*, most states have passed laws preventing such takings in future.

Except . . . in the land or naval forces, or in the Militia

Military personnel do not receive precisely the same guarantees as private citizens. Nevertheless, Congress's rules for the military (authorized by clause 1.8.14) must conform to due process requirements and to 8th Amendment limitations on cruel and unusual punishment.

6th Amendment—Speedy Trial, Counsel

In all criminal prosecutions, the accused shall enjoy the right to a speedy and public trial, by an impartial jury of the State and district wherein the crime shall have been committed; which district shall have been previously ascertained by law, and to be informed of the nature and cause of the accusation; to be confronted with the witnesses against him; to have compulsory process for obtaining witnesses in his favor, and to have the assistance of counsel for his defence.

Incorporation Status of the 6th Amendment

The 6th Amendment names rights so fundamental that they have all been incorporated through the Due Process Clause of the 14th Amendment and therefore apply to the states.

Accused shall enjoy the right to a speedy and public trial

When is a trial not "speedy"? When a judge decides that it's been unduly delayed for no good reason, when the defendant complained about the delay within a reasonable amount of time, and when the delay has been substantial and had a negative impact on the defendant's case. Unless these conditions apply, the 6th Amendment will see the case as "speedy."

As a defendant, be forewarned that your day in Court is unlikely to feel speedy or enjoyable. If, however, your right to a speedy trial has been violated, the judge must dismiss the case.

Public trial

Courts cannot try and convict defendants in secret proceedings shielded from public scrutiny. Fairness requires openness. Nevertheless, trials can be shielded from public view to protect defendants or for various reasons such as national security. They may not be closed more than absolutely necessary.

Impartial jury

The Founding generation saw juries as a vital check on government power. Today we see juries almost entirely in their role in deciding guilt or innocence. But in the eighteenth century, especially in predemocratic Britain, the right and obligation of jury duty was more akin to the right and obligation to vote. Juries made inherently political decisions about what sorts of persons and crimes were worth punishing.

Jury: Nullification

Jurors cannot be punished for their decisions. Colonial American juries often acquitted smugglers and others who ran afoul of English law. Juries have acquitted defendants because they decided the crime was justified. Prior to and during the civil rights movement, all-white juries refused to convict white defendants who committed crimes against nonwhites. The right of jurors to reject the strict letter of the law without punishment was established in English Common Law in 1670. Jurors found William Penn (of Pennsylvania fame) innocent of illegal preaching despite instructions to the contrary from the judge in the case (Bushell's case, 1670). In this important sense, juries reach back to an ancient, predemocratic purpose of giving commoners a limit on the law. See also Peter Zenger's 1735 libel case under the 1st Amendment.

When Do Defendants Have the Right to a Jury Trial?

Trials for crimes punishable by six months or more in prison entitle the defendant to a jury trial. Federal juries must consist of 12 jurors, and their decisions must be unanimous. State juries may consist of six jurors. State juries of 12 may convict by a supermajority. State juries of six may convict only by unanimous vote.

Have the assistance of counsel for his defence

The right to counsel (a lawyer), whether the defendant can afford it or not became incorporated in *Gideon v. Wainright* (1963). Prior to that case, the Court had occasionally ruled that the right to counsel applied only in cases where the defendant was unusually disabled in his or her defense, possibly because of being illiterate.

7th Amendment—Jury Trial

In Suits at common law, where the value in controversy shall exceed twenty dollars, the right of trial by jury shall be preserved, and no fact tried by a jury shall be otherwise reexamined in any Court of the United States, than according to the rules of the common law.

Incorporation Status of the 7th Amendment

This amendment has not been incorporated as a basic liberty that states must accept. But federal judges reviewing cases that began at the state level are restrained by the 7th Amendment from reexamining points of fact.

In Suits at common law

In any civil suit filed at the federal level, defendants have the right to insist on a jury or to waive that right. The jury may have 12 persons (standard) or six persons.

And no fact tried by a jury

On appeal, a judge can set aside a verdict or reduce an award as excessive. But the judge may not challenge the jury's findings of fact. Appellate judges may only examine points of law and due process.

8th Amendment—Cruel and Unusual Punishment

> Excessive bail shall not be required, nor excessive fines imposed, nor cruel and unusual punishments inflicted.

Excessive bail shall not be required

The system allowing defendants to put up bail to guarantee their presence at trial is the product of long tradition. The previous alternative was to detain defendants until trial. The Court has spent little effort on defining "excessive bail." Until 1966, judges were required to give bail for defendants unless they were deemed a flight risk, or if they were accused of a capital crime. In 1984, a new federal law allowed judges to deny bail if defendants were deemed dangerous to the community, and expanded the list of serious crimes that justified denial of bail. The Court upheld that law in *US v. Salerno* (1987).

Nor cruel and unusual punishments inflicted

The prohibition on cruel and unusual punishment was incorporated through the 14th Amendment's Due Process Clause in *Robinson v. California* (1962). From the late 1960s through the early 1980s, the Court made the death penalty more difficult for the states to impose. Since 1987, the Court has steadily made it easier and has declined to rule punishments to be cruel or unusual, or to decide whether punishments are proportionate to the crime.

The Court has struggled to develop a convincing and consistent rule regarding the 8th Amendment's limits on the death penalty and the length of prison sentences, and the question of when the punishment does and does not fit the crime. The Court announced that the Amendment should reflect changing standards of decency, but the meaning of that ruling has remained elusive (*Tropp v. Dulles* [1958]). The Court has asked for additional procedural guarantees for cases regarding the death penalty (*Herrera v. Collins* [1993]).

This amendment has a long history in Anglo-American jurisprudence and is based on a similar clause in the English Bill of Rights of 1689.

9th Amendment—This List of Rights Is Not Complete

> The enumeration in the Constitution, of certain rights, shall not be construed to deny or disparage others retained by the people.

Natural Rights

The framers were concerned that listing rights in the Constitution and Bill of Rights might convey the notion that *only* these rights were to be protected. Americans believed themselves to be endowed with a wide variety of rights, not all of which were mentioned in the Constitution or Bill of Rights. The rights listed and therefore denied to the federal government should not be considered a complete list.

Right to Privacy

In 1965 the Court decided that one of the rights included in the 9th Amendment included the right to privacy. Using the metaphor of a "penumbra" (a sort of shadow), the 1st, 2nd, 3rd, 4th, 5th, and 9th amendments put together, it argued, implied a right to privacy (*Griswold v. Connecticut* [1965]) (Estelle Griswold was executive director of Planned Parenthood in Connecticut). Although the Court has largely abandoned the reasoning that tied the right to privacy to the 9th Amendment, several cases have expanded on the right to privacy based on the Due Process and Equal Protection Clauses of the 14th Amendment (most famously, *Roe v. Wade* [1973]). See below.

Part of the point of the 9th Amendment is to remind us that the American written Constitution has always existed in the prior context of unwritten assumptions regarding the privileges due human beings by virtue of their humanity. That is, the Constitution was written, existed, and exists in the context of a traditional constitutionalism.

10th Amendment—Powers Retained by States, People

> The powers not delegated to the United States by the Constitution, nor prohibited by it to the States, are reserved to the States respectively, or to the people.

Limits on Congress

Put simply, the Bill did not list *all* the limitations on Congress. It did not by implication add any powers to the national government that it had somehow failed to prohibit.

Expressly

This amendment was sometimes understood by states' rights advocates as if it read "The powers not *expressly* delegated to Congress shall be reserved to the states and the people." During the Gilded Age and Progressive Era (1870s–1920s), when the Court was fighting a rearguard battle to stop congressional economic regulation, it agreed with this interpretation. It outlawed the federal Child Labor Act (1916), for example, as interference with states (see *Hammer v. Dagenhart* [1918]). (*Note*: The Articles of Confederation included the term "exclusively" in Clause 2, but the framers deliberately omitted it from the 10th Amendment.)

Decline of the 10th Amendment: "Truism"

In *US v. Darby* (1941) the Court began to treat the 10th Amendment as a truism, as if it did no more than to state the obvious.

Federalist Revival

Starting in *National League of Cities v. Usery* (1976) the Court began to more carefully define rights of the states that, although not listed in the Bill or elsewhere in the Constitution, were not to be infringed on by the Congress. The Court has increasingly argued that, in our system of dual federalism, federal regulations cannot be forced on the states. See *Garcia v. San Antonio Metropolitan Transit Authority* (1985), *New York v. US* (1992), *Printz v. US* (1997), and *US v. Morrison* (2000).

EARLY REFINEMENTS

11th Amendment—States Cannot Be Sued

Proposed March 4, 1794. Ratified February 7, 1795.

The Judicial power of the United States shall not be construed to extend to any suit in law or equity, commenced or prosecuted against one of the United States by Citizens of another State, or by Citizens or Subjects of any Foreign State.

Sovereign Immunity

This amendment overturned the Court's decision in *Chisolm v. Georgia* (1793). In this case, the Court allowed citizens of South Carolina to sue Georgia. Its importance is in how it underlined the sovereign immunity of states and thereby reinforced the system of dual federalism. See *Hans v. Louisiana* (1890) and *Alden v. Maine* (1999).

12th Amendment—Presidential Elections

Proposed December 9, 1803. Ratified June 15, 1804.

The Electors shall meet in their respective states, and vote by ballot for President and Vice President, one of whom, at least, shall not be an inhabitant of the same state with themselves; they shall name in their ballots the person voted for as President, and in distinct ballots the person voted for as Vice President, and they shall make distinct lists of all persons voted for as President, and of all persons voted for as Vice President, and of the number of votes for each, which lists they shall sign and certify, and transmit sealed to the seat of the government of the United States, directed to the President of the Senate;

The President of the Senate shall, in the presence of the Senate and House of Representatives, open all the certificates and the votes shall then be counted; The person having the greatest number of votes for President, shall be the President, if such number be a majority of the whole number of Electors appointed, and if no person have such majority, then from the persons having the highest numbers not exceeding three on the list of those voted for as President, the House of Representatives shall choose immediately, by ballot, the President. But in choosing the President, the votes shall be taken by states, the representation from each state having one vote; a quorum for this purpose shall consist of a member or members from two-thirds of the states, and a majority of all the states shall be necessary to a choice. And if the House of Representatives shall not choose a President whenever the right of choice shall devolve upon them, before the fourth day of March next following, then the Vice President shall act as President, as in the case of the death or other constitutional disability of the President

The person having the greatest number of votes as Vice President, shall be the Vice President, if such number be a majority of the whole number of Electors appointed, and if no person have a majority, then from the two highest numbers on the list, the Senate shall choose the Vice President; a quorum for the purpose shall consist of two thirds of the whole number of Senators, and a majority of the whole number shall be necessary to a choice. But no person constitutionally ineligible to the office of President shall be eligible to that of Vice President of the United States.

Function and History

This amendment replaces clause 2.1.3 because of a problem unforeseen by the framers: political parties. The original plan called for the person with the highest majority of electoral votes to become president, and the person with the second-highest number of votes to become vice president. (See 2.1.3, on the Electoral College, for more details.)

Under the new plan, instead of naming their two top candidates, each elector names a candidate for president and a candidate for vice president.

In the old system, president and vice president might well be from rival parties (this happened with John Adams and Thomas Jefferson in 1796), or party-line electoral votes might result in a tie between president and vice president.

CIVIL WAR AMENDMENTS

The Civil War amendments for the first time *added* to Congress's power and took power away from the states. They gave the national government the power and responsibility to prevent local and state abuses of power. The 13th, 14th, and 15th amendments therefore gave the national government far more power over the states. The Bill of Rights trusted state and local governments and distrusted the national government. The Civil War amendments distrusted state and local governments and trusted the national government.

13th Amendment—Slavery Ended

Proposed January 31, 1865. Ratified December 6, 1865.

Section 1. Neither slavery nor involuntary servitude, except as a punishment for crime whereof the party shall have been duly convicted, shall exist within the United States, or any place subject to their jurisdiction.

Section 2. Congress shall have power to enforce this article by appropriate legislation.

First Reconstruction Amendment

The 13th Amendment ended the right of humans to own each other and added to the power of the federal government through section 2.

Expansive Reading

Republicans at first thought that the 13th Amendment would be the only post–Civil War change to the Constitution. Once slavery was abolished, former slaves would gain civil and political rights. According to the "expansive reading" of the 13th Amendment, Congress's power to enforce an end to slavery also gave Congress power to enforce an end to the "badges and incidents" of slavery such as "Black Codes" and other forms of racial discrimination.

Black Codes

Immediately after the Civil War, states of the former Confederacy began to pass so-called Black Codes to keep former slaves as close to their former condition as possible. These replaced the "Slave Codes."

Civil Rights Act of 1866

Congress confirmed its expansive reading of the 13th Amendment by passing the Civil Rights Act of 1866 over President Andrew Johnson's veto. This act declared all persons born in the US to be citizens of the US and required that they receive the equal protection of the law in all states. At the same time, Congress reauthorized the Bureau of Freedman Affairs, the "Freedman's Bureau," which intervened on the side of former slaves. In both cases, Congress empowered federal officials to enforce national law.

Except as a punishment for crime

Once Reconstruction ended, blacks throughout the South were routinely arrested on fake charges during harvest time so that states could sell their labor as prisoners.

13th Amendment Revived, 1968

Over 100 years after its first passage, the Court overturned
its earlier narrower rulings on the 13th Amendment and
confirmed the more expansive reading. The Civil Rights Act
of 1866 prohibited housing discrimination starting in 1968
(*Jones v. Alfred H. Mayer Co.* [1968]).

14th Amendment—Civil Rights

Summary

In its first incarnation after the Civil War, the 14th Amendment served as a sort of peace treaty with the South. It
required that the national government guarantee liberty
and equality before the law for all Americans in every
state in the country. In the face of Southern resistance in
the Reconstruction era, the 14th Amendment largely lost
this original purpose. It regained elements of its original
function only through the civil rights movement that
took off in the 1950s. Today it is at the center of American
Constitutionalism.

I. Why an Amendment? (Two Crises)
    1. To Stop Extra Votes for the South
    2. To Enforce Racial Equality before the Law
II. Structure of 14th Amendment
    Section 1. States Are Prohibited from Abridging
        a. National Citizenship; National Liberties
        b. Privileges or Immunities
        c. Due Process
        d. Equal Protection under the Law
    Section 2. Penalty for Restricting the Vote
    Section 3. Disqualification for Former Confederates
    Section 4. Repudiation of Confederate War Debt
    Section 5. Power of Enforcement

III. Chronology of 14th Amendment

    1. Post–Civil War: New Birth of Freedom

        a. The *Slaughterhouse Cases* (1873)

        b. The Civil Rights Act of 1875

        c. The *Civil Rights Cases* (1883)

        d. *Plessy v. Ferguson* (1896)

    2. Protection of Economic Freedoms

        a. Substantive Due Process

        b. Women's Health Exception

        c. Economic Regulations Allowed

    3. 1938: Quiet Rediscovery of Civil Rights

    4. 1954: Brown v. Board and the New Birth of Equality

    5. 1970: Affirmative Action and Its Limits

I. Why an Amendment? (Two Crises)

Radical Republicans used the 14th Amendment to address two crises, detailed in the following two sections: (1) to stop extra votes for the South and (2) to enforce racial equality before the law.

1. TO STOP EXTRA VOTES FOR THE SOUTH

After the Civil War, the South was due to reap a windfall of voting power from freed slaves. The 14th Amendment was supposed to stop former slaveholders from controlling that power.

The Three-Fifths Clause (1.2.3) counted state population for each state's House members and Electoral College votes. Before the end of slavery, each slave counted as three-fifths of a person. After the end of slavery, each former slave now counted as five-fifths—a whole person. Ironically, all the slaves who gained their freedom also added to the power of the South by two-fifths of a person. Radical Republicans feared (rightly) that Southern whites would keep this electoral bonus gained by the end of slavery but would prevent former slaves from voting or wielding political power.

2. To Enforce Racial Equality before the Law

Between 1865 and 1868, former Confederates maintained
white supremacy through "Black Codes" and often lethal
violence against black leaders. The various state Black
Codes often required nonwhites to work only in farm jobs
or for yearlong contracts. As in slave times, former slaves in
some states had to get permission to leave the plantation or
be arrested for vagrancy. In short, the Black Codes were an
attempt to return former slaves as closely as possible to the
condition of slavery. The 14th Amendment was a second
attempt to overturn the Black Codes after the 13th Amendment failed to do so.

II. Structure of 14th Amendment

(Five sections listed below.)

Section 1: States Are Prohibited from Abridging

> Proposed June 13, 1866. Ratified July 9, 1868.
>
> All persons born or naturalized in the United States, and
> subject to the jurisdiction thereof, are citizens of the United
> States and of the State wherein they reside. No State shall
> make or enforce any law which shall abridge the privileges
> or immunities of citizens of the United States; nor shall any
> State deprive any person of life, liberty, or property, without
> due process of law; nor deny to any person within its juris-
> diction the equal protection of the laws.

A. National Citizenship; National Liberties

All persons . . . are citizens

In the *Dred Scott v. Sandford* (1857) decision, Justice
Roger B. Taney argued that blacks were automatically
excluded from citizenship. This section of the 14th Amendment directly overturns Taney's ruling. It creates a right

of national citizenship. It overrules the presumption that people become national citizens only to the extent that they become state citizens.

But in the Court's *Slaughterhouse* (1873) opinion, Justice Samuel Miller sought to maintain the balance between national and federal power as it had existed before the Civil War. He read these first two sentences of the 14th Amendment as if they simply restated the existence of state and national citizenship, not as a new standard of national citizenship.

B. Privileges or Immunities

This seems to have been a way of referring generally to constitutional guaranties of liberty, whether stated in the text, in the Bill of Rights, or in Common Law. (See 4.2.1 for parallel language requiring that the "privileges and immunities" of citizens of one state be respected in the others.) The term came from English Common Law, from the social contract ideas of John Locke, and from *Blackstone's Commentaries*. "Immunities" were natural rights that the people did not need to give up to the government in order for it to function. "Privileges" were rights (personal security, liberty, and property) that the government agreed to protect in return for being granted its power by the people. An expansive definition can be found in *Corfield v. Coryell* (1823): "Protection by the government; the enjoyment of life and liberty, with the right to acquire and possess property of every kind, and to pursue and obtain happiness and safety."

In *Slaughterhouse*, the Court ruled that the clause protected only very basic rights such as the right to travel. This narrow definition of the term is why attempts to "incorporate" basic liberties through the 14th Amendment relied on the Due Process Clause. See below.

c. Due Process

No State shall . . . deprive any person

Controversy regarding this phrase centers on the terms
"liberty" and "due process," repeated from the 5th Amendment. The Due Process Clause requires that states respect
due process for *all* persons, whether citizens or not.

Substantive Due Process

See 5th Amendment, above, for discussion of this issue.
After *Slaughterhouse* (1873) narrowed "privileges or immunities," the doctrine of "substantive due process" came
to stand for those liberties such as the right to property that
were so basic that states were forbidden from abridging
them. See below: "III. Chronology of the 14th Amendment,"
under "2. Protection of Economic Freedoms."

d. Equal Protection under the Law

After the Civil War, Southern states' Black Codes singled
out former slaves and free blacks for special punishment
and regulation. This section of the amendment responds directly to the Black Codes. Because of the generous wording
of this term, it would eventually be applied to an increasing
number of classifications (gender, immigrants, ethnicities,
sexuality, ages, religions).

Equal Protection and the Vote

In *Reynolds v. Sims* (1964) the Court made its "one man one
vote" ruling that congressional districts had to be of similar
population. See separate sections on gerrymandering and
congressional districts following 1.2.1, Composition of
House.

2000: Equal Protection and the Vote

Bush v. Gore (2000) ended the recount in the Florida presidential vote on the grounds that ballots were being evaluated according to different criteria in different places. Therefore, the Court argued, it violated equal protection.

Marriage

States have refused to accept some out-of-state marriages because they violated state laws on polygamy, age, or same-sex marriage. But states may not limit marriages in ways that violate the 14th Amendment. *Loving v. Virginia* (1967) overturned Virginia's 1924 anti–mixed race law. As of 2015, the Court also ruled that the 14th Amendment's Due Process and Equal Protection Clauses prohibited states from abridging the right to same-sex marriage (*Obergefell v. Hodges* [2015]).

Section 2: Penalty for Restricting the Vote

Representatives shall be apportioned among the several States according to their respective numbers, counting the whole number of persons in each State, excluding Indians not taxed. But when the right to vote at any election for the choice of electors for President and Vice President of the United States, Representatives in Congress, the Executive and Judicial officers of a State, or the members of the Legislature thereof, is denied to any of the male inhabitants of such State, being twenty-one years of age, and citizens of the United States, or in any way abridged, except for participation in rebellion, or other crime, the basis of representation therein shall be reduced in the proportion which the number of such male citizens shall bear to the whole number of male citizens twenty-one years of age in such State.

Males

This is the first time the term "male" appears in the Constitution.

Irony

This clause should have lowered electoral votes and congressional representation to the extent that a state deprived eligible voters from voting. It was never exercised. Even after Southern states almost entirely disenfranchised blacks, Congress never put this clause into action.

Section 3: Disqualification for Former Confederates

No person shall be a Senator or Representative in Congress, or elector of President and Vice President, or hold any office, civil or military, under the United States, or under any State, who, having previously taken an oath, as a member of Congress, or as an officer of the United States, or as a member of any State legislature, or as an executive or judicial officer of any State, to support the Constitution of the United States, shall have engaged in insurrection or rebellion against the same, or given aid or comfort to the enemies thereof. But Congress may by a vote of two-thirds of each House, remove such disability.

Penalty for Violating Oath to Uphold the Constitution

This was an attempt to prevent former Confederate leaders from taking their old places in the House, Senate, and state governments. It didn't last long. By 1872 Congress applied it only to representatives and senators who served during secession. By 1898 it repealed the penalty entirely.

Section 4: Repudiation of Confederate War Debt

The validity of the public debt of the United States, authorized by law, including debts incurred for payment

of pensions and bounties for services in suppressing insurrection or rebellion, shall not be questioned. But neither
the United States nor any State shall assume or pay any
debt or obligation incurred in aid of insurrection or rebellion against the United States, or any claim for the loss or
emancipation of any slave; but all such debts, obligations
and claims shall be held illegal and void.

Loans to the Confederate States of America Voided

Debt issued in the name of the Confederacy or Confederate states was not to be repaid. For the complexities of this
section, including whether Confederate states ever legally
left the Union, see *Texas v. White* (1869). This section also
erases any ambiguity on whether former slave owners
would be paid for lost human property. They would not.

Section 5: Power of Enforcement

The Congress shall have power to enforce, by appropriate
legislation, the provisions of this article.

By 1883 the Court had narrowed this clause almost out of
existence. See *Civil Rights Cases* (1883), for example.

III. Chronology of the 14th Amendment

The 14th Amendment was a partial success in its first five
years. It's easy to forget. But the Union Army helped to put a
lid on white supremacy over that period. It led to multiracial
legislatures and reform legislation throughout the South.
The white ruling class in the South claimed these Reconstruction governments ruled only with the most rampant
corruption. Historians, however, have found the understand-
able struggles of attempting to govern a postwar society with
a ruined economy, a resistant former ruling class, and newly
empowered groups of poor whites and free blacks.

When the North withdrew troops in 1877, however, the Ku Klux Klan and other white terrorist organizations successfully brought this effort to a halt. After the 1870s, there was little life left in the 14th Amendment. The Court narrowed its first section into near meaninglessness.

By the 1880s the only real meaning left to the 14th Amendment was as a way for the Supreme Court to prevent state legislatures from passing economic regulations. The main liberty it protected was liberty of contract.

The purpose of the 14th Amendment would not return until the civil rights movement won its signal victories in *Brown v. Board of Education* (1954).

1. POST–CIVIL WAR: NEW BIRTH OF FREEDOM

In the first few years after the Civil War, the North sought to fulfill its war aims announced through the Emancipation Proclamation and Lincoln's Gettysburg Address. The Freedman's Bureau advocated for former slaves. Southern slave-era laws forbidding slaves from learning to read were replaced with countless formal and informal schools. The Union Army kept the Ku Klux Klan down with some success.

a. The *Slaughterhouse Cases* (1873)

Even as soon as the end of the 1860s the North had begun to lessen its efforts. The Freedmen's Bureau lost its early leader, Union general William O. Howard (Howard University in Washington, DC, is named after him). The bureau had its budget cut drastically and was defunded by 1872. Up through the mid-1870s, many Southern states saw successful political alliances between former slaves and poor whites. Freedom for the former slaves depended on the willingness of the North to guarantee their political and economic rights against white terrorism by force of arms.

But the Court also had a role in defining those rights. The goals of the 14th Amendment suffered from too much support in 1873 and too little support starting in 1876. In the *Slaughterhouse Cases* (1873), Justice Samuel Miller loved the goals of the 14th Amendment too much. He was a Radical Republican committed to reconstructing the South on racially egalitarian grounds. When New Orleans whites demanded that the Court overturn new laws passed by the state's multiracial legislature, Miller saw it for what it was: an effort to revive white supremacy. A medical doctor himself, Miller wished to support Louisiana's efforts to regulate slaughterhouses. (New Orleans butchers had previously slaughtered and dumped carcasses upstream of the city's water supply.)

Miller's opinion largely returned the guarantee of civil rights to the states, as it had been before the 14th Amendment. This made sense at the time. Miller wished to support the multiracial Reconstruction government of Louisiana.

But Miller's gamble failed when Northerners began to abandon Southern blacks in the mid-1870s (see the Tilden-Hayes Compromise of 1877, which exchanged Republican control of the presidency with an end to Reconstruction) and white supremacists began to take back control of state governments throughout the South. If the Union forces were victorious on the battlefield in 1865, after 1876 the Ku Klux Klan and other groups, often led by former Confederate soldiers, reimposed white supremacy in Southern state governments.

Black leaders and their white supporters were terrorized, humiliated, killed, and exiled. (It is worth noting that blacks and their allies resisted such terrorism in the 1870s and 1880s. When activism became possible again, they and their allies built on the living, if closely held, community memory of early Reconstruction-era triumphs. That community memory came alive in the civil rights movement.)

b. The Civil Rights Act of 1875

The Civil Rights Act of 1875 required equal access to public places such as trains, taverns, and theaters. It relied on the Equal Protection Clause for its power. But the Court struck down this section of the law, arguing that "equal protection" referred only to equality before the law, not to equal access to public spaces that were privately owned (*Civil Rights Cases* [1883]). See *Plessy v. Ferguson* (1896).

c. *Civil Rights Cases* (1883)

The Court ruled that the 14th Amendment protected blacks solely if state governments did the discriminating and explicitly said so. Victims of lynch mobs, Ku Klux Klan members, and other nonstate actors could not turn to the national government for protection. They had to rely on white supremacist state governments. Nor could the national government step in to protect US citizens if state governments refused to protect them. See *US v. Harris* (1882) ("Ku Klux Klan Cases") and *Civil Rights Cases* (1883), in which it overruled the Civil Rights Act of 1875 for similar reasons.

d. *Plessy v. Ferguson* (1896)

Strauder v. West Virginia (1880) made it illegal for states to explicitly pass laws that excluded blacks from jury duty. States had to achieve this goal through less explicit means. *Yick Wo v. Hopkins* (1886) stated that formal equality in a statute did not excuse discrimination in the way it was enforced. (It seemed clear to the Court at the time that the law was being used to exclude Asians from the laundry business.) Although largely ignored at the time, this precedent became more important during the civil rights movement of the 1950s.

Plessy v. Ferguson (1896) ruled that state segregation laws were reasonable as long as they were universal and equal in their scope. They had to equally prohibit different races from mixing. They could not, for example, prohibit blacks from mixing with whites but allow whites to mix with blacks. If black people chose to see such laws as discriminatory, the Court stated, that was their own choice. In practice, "separate but equal" protected only separateness, not equality. *Brown v. Board* (1954) would later (much later) argue that segregation by law implied a judgment of inferiority, and thus, contrary to *Plessy*, segregation laws were inherently unequal. Justice John Marshall Harlan's famous dissent to *Plessy* accused the law's defenders of dishonesty:

> It was said in argument that the statute of Louisiana does not discriminate against either race, but prescribes a rule applicable alike to white and colored citizens. But . . . everyone knows that the statute in question had its origin in the purpose, not so much to exclude white persons from railroad cars occupied by blacks, as to exclude colored people from coaches occupied by or assigned to white persons. . . . No one would be so wanting in candor as to assert the contrary.

Harlan was incorrect about one thing of course: The majority of the Court *was* "so wanting in candor"—that is, it was willing to ignore experience in favor of formal equality. Indeed, the Court's decision in *Plessy* pretended away the history and reality of violent white supremacy.

Plessy v. Ferguson's misleading but temptingly formal balancing act pretended that the violent reality of white supremacy and Jim Crow did not exist. Similarly, Anatole France pointed sarcastically to the majestic formal equality of laws that forbade both rich and poor from sleeping under bridges, so *Plessy* permitted states to pass laws requiring both blacks and whites to accept legal segregation as equal under the Constitution.

2. Protection of Economic Freedoms

After 1873 the Court moved with increasing decisiveness
to create a national standard of citizenship under the 14th
Amendment—for individual property rights. Since the
Slaughterhouse Cases, dissenting Justice Stephen Field had
seen in the 14th Amendment a way to defend the rights of
property against state governments. The states, he thought,
were too tempted to side with farm and labor activists
against railroads, grain silo companies, and the new large-
scale manufacturing and mining businesses.

a. Substantive Due Process

The Court invalidated a state law in *Allgeyer v. Louisiana*
(1897) under the Due Process Clause. The Court had been
moving in this direction for some years but had been slow
to act definitively. In *Munn v. Illinois* (1877) and *Railroad
Commission Cases* (1886) the Court declared that states
could regulate businesses when those businesses engaged in
enterprises "affected with a public interest," but the Court
would judge whether such regulation was reasonable. Starting with *Allgeyer,* and solidifying in *Lochner v. New York*
(1905), the Court declared almost all economic regulations
to be unreasonable.

In this line of cases, the Court protected "liberty of contract" of individual persons against government regulation.
(In *Santa Clara County v. Southern Pacific* [1886] the Court
had declared corporations to be legal persons.)

States were not permitted to pass laws regulating hours
or conditions of labor unless such laws were state "police
power" necessary to protect the health and welfare of their
citizens. Legislators had to show a suspicious Court that
their laws were not intended to protect workers, or to support unions. They had to be passed solely to protect the
health of the public (or to protect particularly at-risk workers such as coal miners. See *Holden v. Hardy* [1898]).

The Court's "liberty of contract" assumed a formal equality between the economic power of the new corporate enterprises and individual employees.

b. Women's Health Exception

In *Muller v. Oregon* (1908), future Court justice Louis D. Brandeis argued that excessive hours for women would undermine the health of the people of Oregon. Therefore, he argued, maximum hours for women should be accepted as a legitimate exercise of state police power. He intended his argument to be an "opening wedge" to insist that too many hours were unhealthy for men, too. (In *Bunting v. Oregon* [1917] the Court upheld such regulations for men as well.) In *Adkins v. Children's Hospital* (1923), the Court refused to apply the argument for *Muller* to minimum wages.

c. Economic Regulations Allowed

With Justice Owen Roberts as the swing vote between Progressives and the conservative "Four Horsemen," the Court had been taking small steps toward overturning its anti–state regulations stance in *Lochner*. (See *Nebbia v. New York* [1934] and *Home Building & Loan Association v. Blaisdell* [1934] for more examples of Court deference to state laws.) But Roberts joined a pro-*Lochner* decision just two years later (*Morehead v. Tipaldo* [1936] overturned a state minimum wage law). Nevertheless, in *West Coast Hotel v. Parrish* (1937), he joined the majority to overrule the liberty of contract precedent of the *Allgeyer/Lochner* era. The Court began to permit "reasonable" state economic regulations.

People at the time called Justice Roberts's vote in favor of the New Deal the "switch in time that saved nine" because it seemed to come in response to President Franklin D. Roosevelt's threat to pack the Court with more justices. It's more complex than that (Roberts changed his vote *before* FDR issued his threat, and the Court had toyed with small changes in 1934), but the impact of FDR's landslide victory in 1936, the real threat that he would indeed pack the Court, and public sentiment that portrayed the Court as a roadblock to progress likely played a role as well.

In this era, the Court also overturned its old interpretation of the Commerce Clause. It now permitted most economic regulations (1.8.3).

3. 1938: Rediscovery of Civil Rights

One year after *West Coast Hotel*, in *Carolene Products* (1938) the Court tentatively rediscovered civil rights. It would now allow almost all *economic* regulations. But it would more carefully scrutinize laws that violated "a specific prohibition of the Constitution, such as that of the first ten amendments," or if they undermined the freedoms of "discrete and insular minorities" (especially if such minorities had limited access to political power). The Court buried its new determination in footnote number 4 of the decision.

Strict Scrutiny: Economic regulations would need pass only minimal scrutiny as having a "rational basis," while those laws that violated the Bill would face "strict scrutiny."

4. 1954: Brown v. Board and the New Birth of Equality

Before *Brown v. Board of Education* (consistent with its "separate but equal" ruling in *Plessy v. Ferguson* [1896] and *Yick Wo v. Hopkins* [1886]), the Court agreed that legally segregated facilities had to be equal in *fact* as well as in formal assumption. Eventually the Court would rule in *Brown* that "separate is inherently unequal."

Brown directly overturned *Plessy* regarding education but also as important overturned the logic of *Plessy* that generally accepted segregation laws as long as they preserved a formal equality. In *Missouri ex rel. Gaines v. Canada* (1938), the Court ruled that when a state provides education for whites, it must provide an equal education for nonwhites. (*Canada* refers to S. W. Canada, the registrar of the University of Missouri, not the nation of Canada.) In *Sweatt v. Painter* (1950) the National Association for the Advancement of Colored People (NAACP) lawyers focused more on whether a new, separate law school for nonwhites could ever truly be "equal." It was a deeply persuasive argument to the law school graduates on the Court, proud as they were of their alma maters. *Sweat*, then, began to press the question of whether separate could *ever* be equal.

The Court ruled in *Brown* that "separate educational facilities are inherently unequal." This May 17, 1954, ruling created "massive resistance" in Southern states that still practiced legal segregation. It would eventually also undermine the long tradition of neighborhood schools in the North, segregated by residential patterns and redlining, and would lead to similar Northern scenes of massive resistance.

The Warren Court of the 1950s and 1960s set itself to a clear task of eliminating government support for racial segregation. *Brown* began the avalanche of rulings that struck down nearly all government-sponsored racial discrimination against blacks. (See also Commerce Clause 1.8.3. The *Heart of Atlanta Motel v. US* [1964] built on the equal rights logic of *Brown* but used the broad grant of economic power gained through the New Deal Commerce Clause to empower Congress to outlaw discrimination in public facilities such as hotels, motels, and restaurants.)

5. 1970–Present: Affirmative Action and Its Limits

The Burger Court of the 1970s found itself saddled with a more difficult problem than its predecessor had. It faced a demand for equality of results and redress of historic discrimination that had created structural inequalities. The civil rights movement's demand for equality of results pointed out the paradox of equality in the Constitution. The Constitution envisioned equality before the law in a society that had long denied it in practice.

But can Congress or the Court do more than avoid discrimination in the present? Using inequality to redress past inequalities is at best a delicate task. As the Court has pointed out, to create special programs to force redress of historic inequalities for African Americans creates new inequalities for present-day Euro-Americans.

Yet proponents of equality argued that the effects of discrimination—hundreds of years of systematically preventing individuals from accessing equal education, good jobs, and political power—meant that simple, blind equality before the laws protected entrenched, structural inequality. To quote a post–Civil War white planter, the end of slavery only meant an end to formal status of humans as property. It gained them "nothing but freedom." That is, they gained nothing but freedom to live in a segregated, white supremacist society without individual savings or the savings of generations, education, credit, or political power. At the time, they also could not count on equality before the law.

The civil rights movement demanded more than merely formal equality. It demanded aggressive efforts to fix the cumulative effects of government policies that had long subsidized white advantage with black disadvantage. For example, after World War II, the GI Bill made it possible for vast new groups of lower-middle-class white families to own their own homes. Over the next few decades, owning their own homes provided whites with the stability of long-term equity. Blacks were redlined out of most of these new suburbs. The GI Bill helped vast new populations of white veterans to attend college, but qualified black students were largely confined to the small number of black institutions of higher learning.

The Court has increasingly taken a dim view of affirmative action, seeing it as another form of unequal protection under the law and pointing to the stigma it may create for its beneficiaries. Chief Justice Roberts wrote in his opinion in a split decision, "The way to stop discrimination on the basis of race is to stop discriminating on the basis of race" (*Parents Involved in Community Schools v. Seattle School District No. 1* [2007]).

The first key case was *Regents of the University of California v. Bakke* (1978). The Court permitted affirmative action to stand only if race was considered in order to rectify past wrongs by the institution in question and was only one of several criteria, individually evaluated. Colleges and universities, the courts ruled, could use holistic criteria (not quotas) to pursue a diverse group of students as a valid and valuable educational goal. The Court has nibbled at this logic in a series of cases but allowed its core to stand (*Grutter v. Bollinger* [2003]).

6. 1973: ABORTION

Until January 1973, abortion was a state matter, outlawed in some states and permitted in others. The debate focused on public health of women and "back alley" abortions. Since *Roe v. Wade* (1973), the debate has shifted to one of competing absolute rights—the right of the fetus to life versus the right of the woman to control her body, and to precisely where one set of rights ends and the other begins. Some argue that life begins at the moment of conception, some when it can survive outside the womb, and some at points in between. After *Roe* was handed down in January 1973, abortion became a 14th Amendment liberty under the Due Process Clause, and based also on the *Griswold v. Connecticut* (1965) case outlining a right to privacy. As abortion has become a matter of right and religion, room for compromise has disappeared.

In *Roe*, the Court ruled that laws regarding a woman's right to make decisions regarding her own health is a paramount liberty, and any state laws regarding that right are subject to "strict scrutiny." At the same time, the government also had a right to protect life before birth. In the first trimester, states are not permitted to regulate a woman's choice of whether or not to abort the fetus. In the second trimester, the states can regulate this choice in ways related to the health of the mother. In the third trimester, the states can regulate abortions. In all of these cases, however, medical judgment regarding the health of the mother must remain primary.

Several states have passed laws attempting to limit access to abortions by imposing waiting periods, requiring doctors to counsel patients on the decision, and outlawing some forms of abortion. The Court has consistently agreed that a woman's right to end her pregnancy is one that may be abridged only at the margins. A small majority of justices have accepted *Roe* as settled law whether they agree with it or not. A solid minority have consistently argued that it should be overturned. A woman's control over whether or not to abort, they argue, should be removed from its status as a paramount 14th Amendment liberty and returned to the states.

Planned Parenthood v. Casey (1992) reaffirms the core reasoning of *Roe*, although it replaces the standard of "strict scrutiny" with "undue burden." *Gonzales v. Carhart* (2007) permits a federal statute outlawing a form of abortion procedure. In 2016 the Court struck down a Texas statute as an "undue burden" on a woman's right to choose an abortion (*Whole Woman's Health v. Hellersted* [2016]).

15th Amendment—Black Men Gain the Vote

Proposed February 26, 1869. Ratified February 3, 1870.

Section 1. The right of citizens of the United States to vote shall not be denied or abridged by the United States or by any State on account of race, color, or previous condition of servitude.

Section 2. The Congress shall have power to enforce this article by appropriate legislation.

Lack of a Federal Bureaucracy

The national government was poorly equipped to enforce regulations when ratified. The 15th Amendment relied on the federal judiciary. The Court was also a slender reed, however. Despite Court rulings, it took development of a federal bureaucracy, a civil rights movement, the Voting Rights Act of 1965, a resurgent Court, and the 24th Amendment (ratified in 1964) outlawing poll taxes to guarantee nonwhites the vote.

Why Wasn't the Right to Vote Part of the 14th Amendment?

Without black votes, advocates didn't have the power in Congress. For the period when Radical Republicans held power after the Civil War, the 14th Amendment gave enough blacks and Northern supporters the vote, for enough time, and with enough support to pass the 15th Amendment.

Impact

Once Reconstruction slowed in 1876, white supremacist state governments used legal tricks short of overt declaration to deny blacks their right to vote. Combined with private primaries for the Democratic Party, one-party (the Democratic Party) rule, and Ku Klux Klan terrorism, if all

else failed, Southern states made the 15th Amendment a
dead letter.

Legal Tricks

One trick was the "Grandfather Clause." All citizens were
required to pass a literacy test unless they or a relative had
been able to vote before Reconstruction. Illiterate white
citizens were therefore able to vote. Local election supervi-
sors invariably disqualified blacks, literate or not. The Court
invalidated literacy tests in *Guinn v. US* (1915). This first
case involving lawyers from the NAACP was something of a
toothless victory. Neither the Court nor any other federal or
state officials took action to enforce it. Other tricks included
poll taxes, segregated political parties, racial gerrymandering, and locally administered tests that supposedly measured constitutional knowledge but actually measured the
administrator's judgment of skin color.

Voting Rights Act of 1965

This act targeted those states with an established prior
record of voter discrimination based on race. From an
initial focus on ensuring that all qualified voters be able to
vote without discrimination, the Court has since turned
its attention toward the acceptable makeup of voting
districts and the question of whether states can establish
a track record of nondiscrimination sufficient to be free
from federal government regulation. See *South Carolina v.
Katzenbach* (1966) for the acceptable reach of federal laws.
See *Allen v. State Board of Election* (1969). In *Shelby County
v. Holder* (2013) the Court freed states from requirements
that they receive preclearance for any changes to voting
rules.

PROGRESSIVE ERA

16th Amendment—Income Taxes

> Proposed July 12, 1909. Ratified February 3, 1913
>
> The Congress shall have power to lay and collect taxes on incomes, from whatever source derived, without apportionment among the several States, and without regard to any census or enumeration.

Income Taxes

This amendment avoided a direct confrontation between Congress and the Court. It responded to the Court's ruling in *Pollock v. Farmers' Loan & Trust Company* (1895). The Court ruled that taxes on any income from property or land were direct taxes and thus had to be apportioned according to a state's level of federal representation (1.2.3).

Direct Tax

Prior to *Pollock*, the Court defined direct taxes narrowly, therefore broadening Congress's taxing powers. From 1862 to 1872 (when the law expired) the US had an income tax. In 1881 the Court ruled that Civil War–era income tax was "indirect." Because it was not a direct tax, it was not covered by clause 1.2.3 or 1.9.4 (*Springer v. US* [1881]).

Income Tax Ruled Unconstitutional

When Congress passed an income tax in 1894, there was little concern at the time regarding its constitutional status. The tax was the product of a widespread Progressive, Populist, and Labor coalition. But the Court struck it down. The Court's decision was broadly seen as a last-ditch defense in a battle between economic class interests. The Court struck down any tax on income from property as a direct tax. (It supposedly authorized income taxes on wages, but since it forbade taxes on any wages derived from property, few wages could really be taxed.)

17th Amendment—Election of Senators by Voters

Proposed May 13, 1912. Ratified April 8, 1913.

Section 1. The Senate of the United States shall be composed of two Senators from each State, elected by the people thereof, for six years; and each Senator shall have one vote. The electors in each State shall have the qualifications requisite for electors of the most numerous branch of the State legislatures.

Section 2. When vacancies happen in the representation of any State in the Senate, the executive authority of such State shall issue writs of election to fill such vacancies: Provided, That the legislature of any State may empower the executive thereof to make temporary appointments until the people fill the vacancies by election as the legislature may direct.

Section 3. This amendment shall not be so construed as to affect the election or term of any Senator chosen before it becomes valid as part of the Constitution.

Popular Election of Senators

Senators were originally selected by state legislatures (see 1.3.1) One of the markers that shifted the Gilded Age to the Progressive Age was the rising chorus against corporate influence in legislatures. The Senate became a symbol of corrupt government.

The 17th Amendment solved several problems with the Senate, as it had come to evolve over the years. By 1911, when the measure passed both House and Senate, over half the states, led by Oregon, had set up ways to achieve popular election of senators. Essentially, they passed laws requiring the legislature to select as senator the winner of a statewide election. The 17th Amendment supplied a formal way for states to fill vacancies midterm if their legislatures gave state governors that power. It also prevented states from substantially narrowing the qualifications for senator.

White Supremacy

A main obstacle to turning popular election of senators from a state-level reform to a formal constitutional amendment was the Southern Democratic whites-only primary system. Since Reconstruction, one way that Southern Democrats had exerted whites-only control over their political system was by confining all political decision making to Democratic primaries. The few African Americans who managed to vote without being lynched could do so only in the Republican primaries, or in the popular elections. To elect senators by popular vote, Southern politicians feared, might allow black voters to have a say in the selection of senators. This fear (unfortunately) proved unfounded.

Filling Vacancies by State Executive

In case of a vacancy, this amendment allows state governors to name a person to serve out the term (if the state legislature so permits them).

18th Amendment—Liquor Outlawed

Proposed December 18, 1917. Ratified January 16, 1919. Repealed by the 21st Amendment, December 5, 1933.

Section 1. After one year from the ratification of this article the manufacture, sale, or transportation of intoxicating liquors within, the importation thereof into, or the exportation thereof from the United States and all territory subject to the jurisdiction thereof for beverage purposes is hereby prohibited.

Section 2. The Congress and the several States shall have concurrent power to enforce this article by appropriate legislation.

Section 3. This article shall be inoperative unless it shall have been ratified as an amendment to the Constitution by the legislatures of the several States, as provided in the Constitution, within seven years from the date of the submission hereof to the States by the Congress.

Revenge of the South and West

This third of four Progressive amendments (16th, 17th, 18th, and 19th) was the first led by the Southern and Western strain of Progressive reform. Starting in 1909 and peaking in 1917, 24 Southern and Western states passed bans on alcohol within their borders. Such bans had little impact on the mint julep supply for the Kentucky Derby but made the purchase of alcohol difficult for poor whites and blacks in the South, and for immigrants in the West. A large number of rural towns and states all over the country followed suit. The national ban on alcohol followed this state-by-state experiment.

Even after repeal, many states, counties, and towns stayed dry or created laws to make purchase of alcohol difficult, or at least annoying.

Unintended Consequences of Prohibition

An amendment intended to make Americans better people promoted lawlessness. Urban and Northern Americans responded with perhaps the largest civil disobedience campaign in American history. Before long, bars in New York City stopped hiding themselves. Organized crime expanded to take advantage of the opportunity. Federal surveillance of ordinary Americans, already given a hard push in the Palmer Raids by US Attorney General A. Mitchell Palmer against Socialists and in attacking antiwar sentiments during World War I, gained another boost for its battles against alcohol. In response to organized crime, the Court vastly expanded the scope of federal law enforcement and surveillance.

19th Amendment—Women Gain the Vote

Proposed June 4, 1919. Ratified August 18, 1920.

The right of citizens of the United States to vote shall not be denied or abridged by the United States or by any State on account of sex. Congress shall have power to enforce this article by appropriate legislation.

The Flip Side of Prohibition?

In 1920 Northern and Western states combined to give women the vote. By this time, most non-Southern states permitted women to vote. The main issue for the South was (as with direct election of senators—see the 16th Amendment) white supremacy in electoral politics. A new federal voting right posed the threat that the national government might begin to regulate voting rights. If so, it might begin to enforce the rights of *black* women and men to vote, as required in the 15th Amendment. They needn't have worried. The federal government did not require Southern states to grant the vote to black women.

NEW DEAL AND POST–WORLD WAR II

20th Amendment—Details about Dates of Office

Proposed March 3, 1932. Ratified January 23, 1933.

(Six sections listed below.)

Section 1. The terms of the President and Vice President shall end at noon on the 20th day of January, and the terms of Senators and Representatives at noon on the 3d day of

> January, of the years in which such terms would have ended
> if this article had not been ratified; and the terms of their
> successors shall then begin.
>
> Section 2. The Congress shall assemble at least once in
> every year, and such meeting shall begin at noon on the 3d
> day of January, unless they shall by law appoint a different
> day.

Adjusting the Timing

Think of this as a bridge between the Progressive amendments and the first flexing of New Deal Democratic muscles. Most of the provisions of the 20th Amendment were first proposed in 1923 at the tail end of the Progressive Era, but it was only passed under the New Deal Democratic Congress of 1932. It fixed timing issues traceable to the slower world of eighteenth-century travel.

Issues

The new United States government began work on March 4, 1789, a date chosen because it gave enough time after ratification for the complex electoral system to work and gave newly elected officials time to make their way to the nation's capital. (The Constitution was ratified as of June 21, 1788.)

Thus, presidents and congressmen stayed in power for four months after an election that they may have lost. Note, too, that the Constitution mandated only one congressional term per year, in December, a full 13 months after the election of a new Congress! Although with the support of majorities of both houses and the president's signature they could and sometimes did meet earlier and more often, they generally met only during the constitutionally mandated periods (see 1.4.2).

Section 3. If, at the time fixed for the beginning of the term of the President, the President elect shall have died, the Vice President elect shall become President. If a President shall not have been chosen before the time fixed for the beginning of his term, or if the President elect shall have failed to qualify, then the Vice President elect shall act as President until a President shall have qualified; and the Congress may by law provide for the case wherein neither a President elect nor a Vice President elect shall have qualified, declaring who shall then act as President, or the manner in which one who is to act shall be selected, and such person shall act accordingly until a President or Vice President shall have qualified.

Section 4. The Congress may by law provide for the case of the death of any of the persons from whom the House of Representatives may choose a President whenever the right of choice shall have devolved upon them, and for the case of the death of any of the persons from whom the Senate may choose a Vice President whenever the right of choice shall have devolved upon them.

Section 5. Sections 1 and 2 shall take effect on the 15th day of October following the ratification of this article.

Section 6. This article shall be inoperative unless it shall have been ratified as an amendment to the Constitution by the legislatures of three-fourths of the several States within seven years from the date of its submission.

Death of President- or Vice President–Elect

Section 3 starts out simple and gets complicated. Simple: If the president-elect dies between the time he or she is elected and noon on January 3, the vice president–elect is automatically to take his or her place as president.

Slightly less simple: If there is a problem with the electoral status of the president-elect, then the vice president–elect shall act as president until the problem is resolved.

Complicated: What happens if neither a president nor a vice president shall have been elected by January 20? Congress shall pass a law naming an acting president until a new president and vice president can be elected. Fortunately, this last provision has never been put to the test. It imagines a situation where the new Congress is sworn in on January 3 and has to rule on who should become president as of noon on January 20, a law that would have to be passed by both houses and signed by the outgoing president.

21st Amendment—Liquor Legalized

Proposed February 20, 1933. Ratified December 5, 1933.

Section 1. The eighteenth article of amendment to the Constitution of the United States is hereby repealed.

Section 2. The transportation or importation into any State, Territory, or possession of the United States for delivery or use therein of intoxicating liquors, in violation of the laws thereof, is hereby prohibited.

Section 3. This article shall be inoperative unless it shall have been ratified as an amendment to the Constitution by conventions in the several States, as provided in the Constitution, within seven years from the date of the submission hereof to the States by the Congress.

Repealed

The 18th Amendment remains the only amendment to the Constitution to be repealed. Its repeal reflects a major shift in American population from South and West to cities, a shift made more radical by the long wait to reapportion House seats to reflect changes in the 1920 census. The

House reflected the more rural population distribution of America's 1910 census until 1929. The census reapportioned 21 seats away from Southern and Western states in 1929.

"Original Package Doctrine" (Packy Run)

The transportation or importation into any State . . .

This section for the first time empowers states to forbid interstate commerce in liquor. Prior to the 18th Amendment, even so-called dry states found it difficult to prevent interstate commerce in liquor. Congressional control over interstate commerce is plenary, and states were forbidden from interfering with it. The original case, *Brown v. Maryland* (1827), ruled that goods imported from one state were not taxable by another until they had been taken out of their original packaging and/or sold. The ruling in *Leisy v. Hardin* (1890) stated that as long as liquor was shipped in its original package, states could not tax or regulate it. (This is the origin of the terms "Package Store" or "Packy Store" or "Packy Run" as they refer to a store selling alcohol.)

Thus, while repealing nationwide Prohibition, the 21st Amendment provided a partial exception to the Commerce Clause (1.8.3) and the Import-Export Clause (1.10.2) to close that pre-Prohibition loophole for thirsty drinkers in dry states.

Local Wineries

Recently the Court has considered whether states have been taking advantage of this clause to protect their local wine makers. Such protectionism is prohibited by implication of a series of Supreme Court cases, the so-called Dormant Commerce Clause. In short, this argument states that the 21st Amendment ending prohibition did not grant states the power to discriminate against out-of-state wineries.

Therefore, states that permit in-state wineries to sell directly
to consumers through the mail must permit out-of-state
wineries to do the same. *Granholm v. Heald* (2005). If Pennsylvania is going to permit wineries from "the Napa Valley
of Pennsylvania" in Berks County to mail bottles of wine
to Pennsylvanians, then it must permit wineries from the
actual Napa Valley of California the same privilege.

22nd Amendment—Two Terms for President

Proposed March 24, 1947. Ratified February 27, 1951.

Section 1. No person shall be elected to the office of the
President more than twice, and no person who has held
the office of President, or acted as President, for more than
two years of a term to which some other person was elected
President shall be elected to the office of the President
more than once. But this Article shall not apply to any
person holding the office of President when this Article
was proposed by the Congress, and shall not prevent any
person who may be holding the office of President, or acting as President, during the term within which this Article
becomes operative from holding the office of President or
acting as President during the remainder of such term.

Section 2. This article shall be inoperative unless it shall
have been ratified as an amendment to the Constitution by
the legislatures of three fourths of the several States within
seven years from the date of its submission to the States by
the Congress.

Term Limits on the President

The 23rd Amendment forces presidents to adhere to George
Washington's rule. Washington remains unusual among
revolutionary leaders in world history for voluntarily
relinquishing power. He resigned after the war, and after a
second term as president announced that he would not run

again. This decision came in part from his wish to go home and from his age. It also came from a desire to embody the republican virtuousness that put public good ahead of private interest. He wished the office to outlive him.

Every president since Washington adhered to this tradition until Franklin D. Roosevelt. FDR's cousin Teddy Roosevelt had also chafed under it.

MOST RECENT

23rd Amendment—Electoral Votes for Washington, DC

Proposed June 16, 1960. Ratified March 29, 1961.

Section 1. The District constituting the seat of Government of the United States shall appoint in such manner as the Congress may direct: A number of electors of President and Vice President equal to the whole number of Senators and Representatives in Congress to which the District would be entitled if it were a State, but in no event more than the least populous State; they shall be in addition to those appointed by the States, but they shall be considered, for the purposes of the election of President and Vice President, to be electors appointed by a State; and they shall meet in the District and perform such duties as provided by the twelfth article of amendment.

Section 2. The Congress shall have power to enforce this article by appropriate legislation.

Presidential Elections and Washington, DC

This amendment did no more than to grant residents of Washington, DC, the right to vote in presidential elections. It did *not* give Washington, DC, any House or Senate representation.

24th Amendment—Poll Tax Prohibited

Proposed August 27, 1962. Ratified January 23, 1964.

Section 1. The right of citizens of the United States to vote in any primary or other election for President or Vice President, for electors for President or Vice President, or for Senator or Representative in Congress, shall not be denied or abridged by the United States or any State by reason of failure to pay any poll tax or other tax.

Section 2. The Congress shall have power to enforce this article by appropriate legislation.

Limited to Federal Elections Only

Note that this amendment applied only to federal elections. The Constitution largely leaves management of elections to the states.

Pay to Vote

The Court ruled that all citizens had the right to vote in all local elections as well, whether they had paid their taxes or not (*Harper v. Virginia Board of Electors* [1966]).

25th Amendment—Presidential Succession

Proposed July 6, 1965. Ratified February 10, 1967.

(Four sections listed below.)

Section 1. In case of the removal of the President from office or of his death or resignation, the Vice President shall become President.

Section 2. Whenever there is a vacancy in the office of the Vice President, the President shall nominate a Vice President who shall take office upon confirmation by a majority vote of both Houses of Congress.

Rules of Succession

The following presidents have died in office and been replaced by their vice presidents: William Henry Harrison (1841), Zachary Taylor (1850), Abraham Lincoln (1865), William McKinley (1901), Warren G. Harding (1923), Franklin D. Roosevelt (1945), and John F. Kennedy (1963). In each case, the sitting vice president rose to the presidency as laid out in the rule of succession in clause 2.1.6.

Selecting a New Vice President

Section 2 solves the problem of filling the office of vice president between elections. Prior to this, when vacated for any reason, including promotion to president, the office of vice president would remain vacant until the next election. The lack of a vice president did not cripple the government, but it raised the issue of succession, should the new president also become incapacitated or removed from office between elections.

Section 3. Whenever the President transmits to the President pro tempore of the Senate and the Speaker of the House of Representatives his written declaration that he is unable to discharge the powers and duties of his office, and until he transmits to them a written declaration to the contrary, such powers and duties shall be discharged by the Vice President as Acting President.

Section 4. Whenever the Vice President and a majority of either the principal officers of the executive departments or of such other body as Congress may by law provide, transmit to the President pro tempore of the Senate and the Speaker of the House of Representatives their written declaration that the President is unable to discharge the powers and duties of his office, the Vice President shall immediately assume the powers and duties of the office as Acting President.

Thereafter, when the President transmits to the President pro tempore of the Senate and the Speaker of the House of Representatives his written declaration that no inability exists, he shall resume the powers and duties of his office unless the Vice President and a majority of either the principal officers of the executive department or of such other body as Congress may by law provide, transmit within four days to the President pro tempore of the Senate and the Speaker of the House of Representatives their written declaration that the President is unable to discharge the powers and duties of his office. Thereupon Congress shall decide the issue, assembling within forty-eight hours for that purpose if not in session. If the Congress, within twenty-one days after receipt of the latter written declaration, or, if Congress is not in session, within twenty-one days after Congress is required to assemble, determines by two-thirds vote of both Houses that the President is unable to discharge the powers and duties of his office, the Vice President shall continue to discharge the same as Acting President; otherwise, the President shall resume the powers and duties of his office.

Voluntary Incapacity

In case the President decides he or she cannot perform his or her duties for any reason, the vice president becomes acting president. The president so notifies the House and Senate of this decision, and it remains in force until the president rescinds it. When Reagan underwent a surgical operation, he wrote to both the Speaker of the House and to the president pro tempore of the Senate, declaring that Vice President George Bush would be acting president during the medical procedure. Nevertheless, he chose not to invoke this clause of the 25th Amendment. In 2002 and 2007 President George W. Bush invoked this clause of the 25th Amendment for brief periods while he underwent medical procedures. In each case, Vice President Dick Cheney became acting president.

Involuntary Removal

But what if the president is so incapacitated as to be unable (or unwilling) to so notify House and Senate? In this case, the vice president together with the majority of the Cabinet makes this decision.

If removed involuntarily, the president may notify Congress that he or she is ready to resume office, essentially appealing this decision by the vice president and majority of the Cabinet. If the vice president and Cabinet agree that the president is capable of serving, the president immediately resumes his or her duties. If they disagree, they have four days to so notify Congress, and Congress may agree by two-thirds vote. If so, then the vice president remains in office as acting president. Congress has 21 days to make this decision. Otherwise, the president resumes his or her duties.

26th Amendment—18-Year-Olds Gain the Vote

Proposed March 23, 1971. Ratified July 1, 1971.

Section 1. The right of citizens of the United States, who are eighteen years of age or older, to vote shall not be denied or abridged by the United States or by any State on account of age.

Section 2. The Congress shall have power to enforce this article by appropriate legislation.

Why Give 18-Year-Olds the Vote?

In his 1954 State of the Union speech, President Dwight D. Eisenhower devoted an entire section to suffrage. He recommended that Congress take action to grant the vote to the people of the District of Columbia, and that Hawaii be granted statehood. He asked that the states allow their overseas soldiers an easier way to vote. He also asked for a constitutional amendment allowing 18-year-old citizens to vote. He explicitly put this request in the context of

18-year-old citizens being called on to serve in the military. If they are to be asked to fight, he argued, they should have the right to participate politically in the decisions that cause them to risk their lives.

Federal versus State Suffrage

In 1970, pressed by the unpopularity of the Vietnam War, Congress passed a law lowering the voting age for all elections at all levels. The 26th Amendment came as a response to the Court's narrow rule in *Oregon v. Mitchell* (1970) that Congress could not regulate state voting ages by law. See clause 1.2.1, which gives states the power to rule on the qualifications of electors.

27th Amendment—Congressional Pay Raises Limited

> Proposed September 25, 1789. Ratified May 7, 1992.
>
> No law, varying the compensation for the services of the Senators and Representatives, shall take effect, until an election of Representatives shall have intervened.

Pay Raises and Emoluments

This amendment fits nicely with the Emoluments Clause, 1.6.2, which prevents lawmakers from holding additional jobs, or from leaving to take jobs that had been created or that had their pay raised since the lawmaker had been in office.

This amendment is an oddity in that it was proposed as one of the original Bill of Rights but not ratified by a sufficient number of states. Since there was no explicit time limit on its passage, a college student who had researched the subject for a paper decided to campaign for its passage. He was more successful with his campaign than with the original paper, which received a "C" grade.

CONCLUSION

The American Creed

The United States Constitution begins with the words "We the People," and Americans to this day battle over whom those words include. Who is entitled to the Constitution's guarantees of liberty and equality? It is a crucial national conversation, for the Constitution cannot enforce itself.

The past half-century has seen a massive shift in who has full political status as a member of "the People." Full political participation for nonwhites and for women began in earnest only in the 1960s. American political customs and institutions have yet to entirely catch up with these changes. Hence, America still finds itself in a slow-moving constitutional crisis. The history of American constitutionalism matters in the ongoing resolution of that crisis.

In 1776 the Declaration of Independence insisted that "all men are created equal." After the Revolutionary War, Independence Day gatherings toasted the equality of all men, no matter their level of wealth. At the time, toasters could ignore the question of whether "all men" included all people, no matter their gender or race.

Soon, however, African American and woman activists changed the conversation. They claimed the Declaration's promise of equality for themselves. The Colored Men's Conventions that began in the 1830s and the Seneca Falls Convention of 1848 argued that the Declaration made a promise of equality and that the nation had failed to fulfill it.

In his 1863 Gettysburg Address, Abraham Lincoln agreed. He argued that the Declaration of Independence promised a constitution that included all men, regardless of race. To him, the Constitution was but an imperfect attempt to enact the ideals of the Declaration, and the Civil War an effort to better achieve that promise.

Just after the Civil War, the 14th Amendment enshrined Lincoln's argument within the Constitution. More than that, the 14th Amendment required the national government to actively guarantee equality and liberty for "the People" regardless of race.

For roughly a decade, the national government enforced the 14th Amendment. In those years, former slaves gained the status of full citizenship and protection from the national government. By 1877, however, the national government abandoned the goals of the 14th Amendment. It gave in to pressure from a terrorist white supremacist movement in the South and from racist assumptions in the North. After 1877 the national government permitted nonwhites to be excluded from "the People" of the Constitution.

By the 1880s, little remained of the goals Lincoln announced at Gettysburg. For nearly a hundred years, Americans ignored the plain language of the 14th Amendment.

Only one main point survived in the 14th Amendment, and it was one that the Court had to invent: individual liberty of contract. The Court used the 14th Amendment to prohibit states from passing laws that set maximum hours, minimum wages, permitted labor unions, or prohibited child labor.

But for many Americans, especially African Americans, women, and wage workers, a strictly individual liberty of contract perverted the nation's promises of equality and human rights. To them, equality and liberty meant a positive national commitment to laws that would bring an end to mob violence and lynching. It meant government protection, legal equality, and the vote. It meant the right to organize and to bargain as groups free from the violence of private police forces and the right of states to pass laws to protect the health and safety of their people.

Only in the 1920s and 1930s did all Americans begin to achieve these goals.

A formidable women's movement achieved the vote through the 19th Amendment in 1920. The phrase in the Declaration that "all men are created equal" began to sound more like "All *people* are created equal."

During the Great Depression of the 1930s, the Court began to permit Congress and state legislatures to pass economic regulations and to allow collective bargaining. It broadened Congress's power under the Commerce Clause to pass almost any regulations related to the economy.

In 1935 the National Association for the Advancement of Colored People began its long legal campaign to revive the goals of the 14th Amendment through the courts.

In World War II, African Americans fought the "Double V" campaign for Victory abroad and Victory at home. Lynchings increased when black soldiers returned after both World War I and World War II.

Nevertheless, despite the renewal of white terrorism, the civil rights movement changed the national conversation about who deserved full citizenship. It used creative protests, boycotts, and political activism, and it taught activists of all stripes how to bring their ideas into the public arena. It explicitly framed American politics as a battle over who was entitled to full status under the Constitution.

In the 1954 *Brown v. Board of Education* case, the Court finally ruled that the 14th Amendment meant what it said about equality and liberty. Strictly speaking, the ruling only applied to public education, but the logic of *Brown* also exposed the unconstitutional nature of all racist laws.

Nine years later, and almost exactly one hundred years after Lincoln at Gettysburg, Martin Luther King Jr. brought the promise of equality and liberty for all Americans into the modern era. His 1963 "I Have a Dream" speech referred back to the promises of Abraham Lincoln's 1863 Gettysburg Address and Thomas Jefferson's 1776 Declaration of Independence. He called for economic as well as racial liberties. In a modern world, he argued, liberty and equality required equal access to jobs and justice.

Within a few years the United States Congress passed a series of laws and a Constitutional Amendment to end interpretations of the Constitution that permitted racism. It passed the Civil Rights Act of 1964, the 24th Amendment that outlawed poll taxes in federal elections, the Voting Rights Act of 1965, and the Education Amendments Act of 1972. (Generally referred to as "Title IX," this latter act required an end to discrimination by gender in publicly funded schools.)

The civil rights movement changed the internal workings of American constitutionalism. It effectively gave full constitutional status to all Americans.

Today, the 14th Amendment binds American constitutional liberties to all state and local governments. Originally, the Bill of Rights bound Congress only. As the Court takes the implications of the 14th Amendment more seriously for more categories of people, it has begun to insist that the national government enforce more of the liberties named in the Bill of Rights in every state and local government for all Americans.

America is still a young nation. As a nation that grants all of its people full status, it is even younger. It has had only a few hundred years to develop customs of governance. It has almost exactly one century of including women as full members of "the People." Only since the 1960s have African

Americans begun to gain that status. And only recently have Americans grappled with full constitutional status around gender and sexuality.

America is still struggling today with how to govern itself under these new rules. The nation has finally defined "the People" of our Constitution in a way that begins to do full justice to the promise of the Declaration of Independence and the egalitarian spirit of the Revolution. But it is still re-creating cultural and political assumptions for a constitutional system that no longer permits old habits of inequality.

The United States does not have the luxury of basing itself on ancient tradition, shared ethnicity, or an established religion. It is a post-tribal nation. It bases itself on a shared political culture that accepts the legitimacy of the Constitution and of governing institutions.

Yet political legitimacy is a fragile thing. This is why Supreme Court justices must care so much about tending historical chains of precedent. This is why presidents, senators, and members of Congress must treat history and custom with reverence and each other with formal courtesy. This is why congressional districts must feel to voters more like stable political entities for choosing members of Congress and less like political entities for members of Congress to choose voters. This is why we need elections that reflect debate and a process of building agreement and consensus.

The current constitutional crisis is why we so need a healthy civil society, broad political participation, and activist organizations. Modern American constitutionalism assumes widespread participation at every level of politics. The Constitution quietly assumes an unbroken complex of connections in our political culture from towns through county, state, and national government systems. The vast network of American politics requires people to work together at every level. It requires people who circulate petitions and hold political meetings in their living rooms. It includes small-town mayors, members of town councils, planning commissions, school boards, and parks committees. Post–civil rights politics is a vastly complicated web that extends well beyond political parties into our civil society.

The constitutional system of the United States is more than a text. It is a crucial national project in which all Americans have a stake. Today a radically larger proportion of all Americans count as the People of the Constitution than ever before. As Lincoln reminded the world at Gettysburg, Americans have fought and died for a constitutional culture capable of achieving the goals of the Revolution. Americans have an obligation to ensure that, in Lincoln's words, "these dead shall not have died in vain, that this nation under God shall have a new birth of freedom, and that government of the people, by the people, for the people shall not perish from the earth."

Constitutional Quotations

Rabbi Hillel, Tenth Century

That which is hateful to you do not do unto your neighbor. That is the entire Bible. All the rest is commentary. Go and study it.

Article 39 of the Magna Carta, 1215

No free man shall be seized or imprisoned, or stripped of his rights or possessions, or outlawed or exiled, or deprived of his standing in any other way, nor will we proceed with force against him, or send others to do so, except by the lawful judgement of his equals or by the law of the land.

Thomas Jefferson et al., Declaration of Independence, 1776

When in the Course of human events, it becomes necessary for one people to dissolve the political bands which have connected them with another, and to assume among the powers of the earth, the separate and equal station to which the Laws of Nature and of Nature's God entitle them, a decent respect to the opinions of mankind requires that they should declare the causes which impel them to the separation. We hold these truths to be self-evident, that all men are created equal, that they are endowed by their Creator with certain unalienable Rights, that among them are Life, Liberty and the pursuit of Happiness.

Address to the Free People of Colour of these United States, 1830

. . . all men are born free and equal, and consequently are endowed with unalienable rights, among which are the enjoyments of life, liberty, and the pursuits of happiness. Viewing these as incontrovertible facts, we have been led to the following conclusions; that our forlorn and deplorable situation earnestly and loudly demand of us to devise and pursue all legal means for the speedy elevation of ourselves and brethren to the scale and standing of men.

Declaration of Sentiments, Seneca Falls Convention, 1848

We hold these truths to be self-evident: that all men and women are created equal; that they are endowed by their Creator with certain inalienable rights; that among these are life, liberty, and the pursuit of happiness . . .

Abraham Lincoln, Gettysburg Address, November 1863

Fourscore and seven years ago our fathers brought forth on this continent a new nation, conceived in liberty and dedicated to the proposition that all men are created equal . . .

John Bingham et al., 14th Amendment to the US Constitution, 1868

All persons born or naturalized in the United States, and subject to the jurisdiction thereof, are citizens of the United States and of the State wherein they reside. No State shall make or enforce any law which shall abridge the privileges or immunities of citizens of the United States; nor shall any State deprive any person of life, liberty, or property, without due process of law; nor deny to any person within its jurisdiction the equal protection of the laws.

Martin Luther King, "I Have a Dream" Speech, August 1963

In a sense, we've come to our nation's capital to cash a check. When the architects of our Republic wrote the magnificent words of the Constitution and the Declaration of Independence, they were signing a promissory note to which every American was to fall heir. This note was a promise that all men—yes, black men as well as white men—would be guaranteed the unalienable rights of life, liberty, and the pursuit of happiness.

Acknowledgments

In a book designed to fit in a pocket, errors of omission are inevitable. Please accept my apologies for leaving out your favorite key cases and issues.

Errors of commission are less inevitable, though some may be less errors and more differences between my opinion and yours. I hope you will at least find that I have done partial justice, or at least minimal violence, to the insights of those whose efforts preceded my own. Or at least that my work here represents an honest effort to get it right.

Thanks are due to Richard Brown and the staff of Georgetown University Press for their support of this edition of the book.

Thank you as well to my students. Every year we talk our way through the history of the Constitution, and every year I learn something new. Our conversations have informed this book.

Thank you to my parents, Jane and Dan Arnold. My views on American constitutionalism have been informed by my experience of watching them take part in the innumerable boards, commissions, and volunteer organizations that make municipalities into recognizable political communities. It is this kind of service that the Constitution quietly assumes and that animates so much of the hidden infrastructure of American politics. My mother served as justice of the peace, and my father served as a member of the school board. My father batted ninth for the local Republican Party softball team. I remember putting up election posters with my father and watching my mom mock up the *Bloomfield ZIP* newspaper as its founder and first editor.

Thank you to my local community here in Kutztown. I have
served on the Borough of Kutztown's Planning Commission, the Housing License Appeals Board, and as president
of the Kutztown Community Partnership, an organization
that promotes what Kutztown has to offer as well as its links
to the school district and Kutztown University. A few years
ago I lost an election to Borough Council by 29 votes.

To my family, Arabel, Sam, and Sophie, I am grateful
beyond words for the life that lets me do things like write
a book on the Constitution. We only moved here in 2002.
Even though we are not Pennsylvania Dutch, we have been
accepted here, and Sam and Sophie view themselves as
natives. In fall 2017 Arabel won a spot on the Kutztown
Borough Council. She took office in January 2018.

Bibliography

REFERENCE BOOKS AND PRIMARY SOURCES

Max Farrand, *The Records of the Federal Convention of 1787*, 4 vols. New Haven, CT: Yale University Press, 1987.
> This four-volume documentary history is invaluable for those who truly wish to investigate the Constitutional Convention itself and the thinking of the framers at the time. It includes most known notes and other materials from and about the Convention. It's available in electronic form online, although it is far more interesting to dip into in bound form. Use the 1987 edition for index, bibliography, and additional material in volume 4.

Federalist Papers (available in different editions and online).
> These are articles published anonymously by Alexander Hamilton, James Madison, and John Jay to support ratification of the Constitution.

Anti-Federalist Papers.
> These are less-well-known essays opposing ratification of the Constitution.

FindLaw is a reference site on American law. www.findlaw.com.

The official site of the US Supreme Court is www.supremecourtus.gov. From here you can download recent opinions and gather additional information.

The Avalon Project is an amazing collection of legal documents going back to the beginning of recorded human history. Publicly available at http://avalon.law.yale.edu.

The ConSource project contains documents and sources on the Constitution. www.consource.org.

J-Stor is a paid site that gives full-text access to thousands of scholarly journal articles. If you are at a college or university, you should already have access. www.jstor.org.

LexisNexis is a terrific if expensive resource for up-to-date access to court rulings and news. www.lexisnexis.com.

Sue Davis, ed. *Corwin and Peltason's Understanding the Constitution*, 17th ed. Belmont, CA: Thomson/Wadsworth, 2008.
    This is still the most affordable complete reference.

Leonard Levy, Kenneth L. Karst, and Dennis J. Mahoney, eds. *Encyclopedia of the American Constitution*, 4 vols., 2nd ed. Macmillan, 2000.

Constitutional Law Casebooks are used to teach the Constitution to law students. There are many available, new and used. Most have over 1,000 pages. These are particularly useful for a sense of how lawyers think.

BOOKS ON THE CONSTITUTION

The following are books for nonspecialists. Hopefully these books will lead you to others on the subject.

Akhil Reed Amar, *America's Constitution: A Biography*. New York: Random House, 2006.

———. *Bill of Rights: Creation and Reconstruction*. New Haven, CT: Yale University Press, 2000.

Michael Les Benedict, *The Blessings of Liberty: A Concise History of the Constitution of the United States*. Lanham, MD: Rowman & Littlefield, 2016.
    Note: This is a textbook.

Catherine Drinker Bowen, *Miracle at Philadelphia: The Story of the Constitutional Convention.* Boston: Back Bay, 1986.

> This book is probably the most accessible on the list, a classic assigned in high schools and colleges for many years; it creates a dramatic narrative of the summer of 1787.

Michael Kent Curtis, *No State Shall Abridge: The Fourteenth Amendment and the Bill of Rights.* Durham, NC: Duke University Press, 1990.

Joseph Ellis, *Founding Brothers: The Revolutionary Generation.* New York: Knopf, 2013.

Don E. Fehrenbacher, *Slavery, Law, and Politics: The Dred Scott Case in Historical Perspective.* Oxford: Oxford University Press, 1981.

Paul Finkelman and Melvin Urofsky, *A March of Liberty: A Constitutional History of the United States*, Vol. 1: *From the Founding to 1900*; and Vol. 2, *From 1898 to the Present.* Oxford: Oxford University Press, 2011.

Barry Friedman, *The Will of the People: How Public Opinion Has Influenced the Supreme Court and Shaped the Meaning of the Constitution.* New York: Farrar, Straus and Giroux, 2009.

Francis Fukuyama, *The Origins of Political Order: From Prehuman Times to the French Revolution.* New York: Farrar, Straus and Giroux, 2011.

Jack P. Greene, *Peripheries and Center: Constitutional Development in the Extended Polities of the British Empire and the United States, 1607–1788.* London: University of Georgia, 1986.

Paul Kens, *Lochner v. New York: Economic Regulation on Trial.* Lawrence: University Press of Kansas, 1998.

Alex Keyssar, *The Right to Vote: The Contested History of Democracy in the United States*, rev. ed. New York: Basic Books, 2009.

David E. Kyvig, *Explicit and Authentic Acts: Amending the U.S. Constitution, 1776–1995*. Lawrence: University Press of Kansas, 1998.

Leonard W. Levy, *Origins of the Bill of Rights*. New Haven, CT: Yale University Press, 2001.

———. *Origins of the Fifth Amendment: The Right against Self-Incrimination*. New York: Oxford University Press, 1968. Reprint, Chicago: Ivan R. Dee, 1999.

Anthony Lewis, *Make No Law: The Sullivan Case and the First Amendment*. New York: Vintage, 1992.

Jack N. Rakove, *Original Meanings: Politics and Ideas in the Making of the Constitution*. New York: Vintage, 1997.

Michael A. Ross, *Justice of Shattered Dreams: Samuel Freeman Miller and the Supreme Court during the Civil War Era*. Baton Rouge: Louisiana State University Press, 2003.

Mark Tushnet, *A Court Divided: The Rehnquist Court and the Future of Constitutional Law*. New York: Norton, 2005.

Melvin I. Urofsky, *Dissent and the Supreme Court: Its Role in the Court's History and the Nation's Constitutional Dialogue*. New York: Vintage Books, 2017.

Garry Wills, *Lincoln at Gettysburg: The Words That Remade America*. New York: Simon & Schuster, 1992.

Gordon Wood, *Radicalism of the American Revolution*. New York: Vintage, 1993.

Index